HANDBOOK TO HAPPINESS

HANDBOOK
to Happiness

DR. CHARLES R.
SOLOMON

Tyndale House Publishers, Inc.
WHEATON, ILLINOIS

Designed by Melinda Schumacher

Edited by Susan Taylor

This book was originally published under the title *Handbook of Happiness* by House of Solomon, Denver, Colorado. The first edition by Tyndale House Publishers, Inc., was done by arrangement with House of Solomon.

The material in this book may be used by laymen and pastors in sharing with others how their deepest needs may be met. It is not to be used in any professional counseling office or practice advertised as Spirituotherapy except as duly authorized by Grace Fellowship International, P.O. Box 368, Pigeon Forge, TN 37868. You may visit the GFI Web site at www.SolomoNet.org.

The poems originally published in the first edition may now be found, along with a number of others, in books published by Solomon Publications entitled, *Handbook to Happiness in Verse, The Ins and Out of Rejection,* and *The Rejection Syndrome and the Way to Acceptance.*

Unless otherwise indicated, Scripture quotations are taken from the *Holy Bible,* King James Version.

Scripture quotations marked NIV are taken from the *Holy Bible,* New International Version®. NIV®. Copyright © 1973, 1978, 1984 by International Bible Society. Used by permission of Zondervan Publishing House. All rights reserved.

Scripture quotations marked TLB are taken from *The Living Bible* copyright © 1971. Used by permission of Tyndale House Publishers, Inc., Wheaton, Illinois 60189. All rights reserved.

Other books by Dr. Solomon:

The Ins and Out of Rejection

Handbook for Christ-Centered Counseling

The Rejection Syndrome and the Way to Acceptance

Gems and Jargon

Handbook to Happiness in Verse

Handbook to Happiness and You—A Spiritual Clinic

All are available from Solomon Publications, P.O. Box 6115, Sevierville, TN 37864. E-mail: chuckgfi@aol.com

Library of Congress Cataloging-in-Publication Data

Solomon, Charles R.

    Handbook to happiness / Charles R. Solomon. — Rev. & updated.
      p. cm.
    Includes bibliographical references (p.   ).
    ISBN 0-8423-1809-7 (pbk. : alk. paper)
    1. Pastoral counseling.   2. Counseling. I. Title.
BV4012.2.S65   1999
253.5—dc21   99-34774

Printed in the United States of America

05   04   03   02   01

7   6   5   4   3

To my wife, Sue,
who has shared and suffered with me
as my life was shaped on God's anvil
that I might begin to be
"conformed to his image"

(ROM. 8:29).

Contents

Heart to Heart

When we come to the place of full retreat
And our heart cries out for God,
The only person whose heart ours can meet
Is one who has likewise trod.

Others may offer a word of cheer
To lift us from despair;
But above the rest, the one we hear
Is the whisper, "I've been there."

Charles R. Solomon

Foreword

I welcome the opportunity to write this brief foreword to Dr. Charles Solomon's revised and expanded book *Handbook to Happiness*. What first drew me to his "counseling ministry" was his philosophy based on his theology! His contention is that many psychological problems are rooted in spiritual problems that can be resolved by a faith union with Christ, crucified, risen, and active in the believer's life. Dr. Solomon knows that my life's verse is Galatians 2:20. In fact, I have written a book titled *Not I but Christ*.

We do not overlook, of course, the place and profession of the psychologist or psychiatrist. Certain distresses and diseases require medical and clinical diagnosis and treatment. So I thank God for outstanding Christian men and women who have been trained to serve in these fields of holistic healing.

Supplementary to this, however, are the multitudes of people in desperate need who are being helped and healed by Spirituotherapy. Therefore, I commend this approach to counseling for three simple reasons: First the counseling is *biblical*. God says: "I am the Lord, who heals you" (Exodus 15:26, NIV). The reference here is to God's healing power both physically and morally in total response to his commands and statutes. Something miraculous and marvelous happens when the Word of God is taught, applied, and obeyed. The psalmist could declare, "[God] sent his word, and healed them" (Psalm 107:20). This, essentially, is the ministry of Dr. Solomon. Depressed and defeated people come to him, and they go away healed by the living Word of God.

Second, the counseling is *balanced*. Reading through this book once again, I sensed the balanced approach to this vital ministry of helping and healing people's minds and bodies. Dr. Solomon does not claim a monopoly in his methodology; he recognizes that some patients require more than what he can offer. I am always skeptical of those who claim to be the "only" answer to human need.

Third, the counseling is *beneficial*. I invite readers to peruse these pages and examine the testimonies of those who have been personally and eternally benefited by the doctor's ministry. He calls these personal records God's faithful interventions. And, to say the least, they ring true.

As this new edition of *Handbook to Happiness* goes forth, I pray that God will greatly use it to bring many into the experience of miraculous and victorious living, to the glory of God!

Stephen F. Olford
Founder of the Stephen Olford Center for Biblical Preaching
Memphis, Tennessee

Preface

It has now been twenty-eight years since I wrote the first edition of this book. I believe it is time to update it and add material that supplements and substantiates its message. Since I had been counseling less than two years when I wrote the first edition, the number of lives impacted was fewer, and the influence of the ministry was limited to the state of Colorado.

The original first chapter, revised and updated, now appears at the end of the book, since some stumbled over the psychological terminology in the first edition and gave up on the book. Some have objected to my taking a firm stand relative to approaches to counseling that are not centered on the believer's relationship to the cross of Christ. Others have said that I was too lenient in exposing the degree to which secular and humanistic thinking have influenced accepted norms in Christian psychology and psychiatry today. However, some who have led the integrationist movement are now having second thoughts, such that a reformation in Christian counseling may be imminent—indeed, absolutely necessary—if Christian counseling is to survive in the new millennium.

I realize that mine is decidedly the minority opinion. Yet it is a conviction given by God. And, as with Luther in the Reformation, I must stand true to the illumination I have received and let those who object sort out their convictions for themselves. Obviously, those who have opted for a more psychological approach, those who object to a theology that holds to the necessity of what we will in this book describe as "the exchanged life" and "the experienced cross" will never be friends with this approach.

Over the years God has called many others to share in the ministry, and the Spirit of God has touched literally thousands of lives in this and other countries. Some of those whose lives have been transformed had been defeated Christians. Some were lost and then were found by the Savior. Others had suffered debilitating emotional disturbances, and many had difficulties with interpersonal relationships. Many of these would have been classified as severely neurotic, and some had been labeled psychotic, though we do not use such labels in our dealing with people in spiritual ministry.

Several states and foreign countries now have counseling and training centers. Grace Fellowship International (GFI) has directly established works in Indiana, Missouri, Georgia, Florida, and Tennessee; and a number of spin-off ministries developed around the country have been greatly used of God.

In addition to the ministries in this country, there are now centers in Argentina, India, and South Africa. Training in varying degrees has now been done on six continents. Contacts are using the materials in Canada, Nigeria, Kenya, Malawi, Zambia, Tanzania, Uganda, Ghana, throughout Latin America, Korea, Japan, Australia, Nepal, Myanmar (Burma), the Philippines, China, the United Kingdom, Belgium, France, Germany, Austria, Switzerland, Russia, Hungary, Romania, Spain, and elsewhere.

Handbook to Happiness has been published in Spanish and in two translations in Korean. An English edition has also been published in India. Chapter 2 has been translated into more than fifteen languages and has been condensed into tract form ("Wheel and Line," available from Solomon Publications) for use in personal work. Several other language editions are in process, the publication of which will make it possible to introduce the message and methods of Spirituotherapy into other strategic parts of the world. The English version is on our Web site at www.SolomoNet.org, and we are presently adding it in nine other main languages of the world.

In the beginning the ministry was limited to counseling as a means of propagating the truth of freedom through union with Christ in his death and resurrection. We found it necessary to prove to critics of this method that a viable integration of counseling and

the Word of God done in the power of the Holy Spirit (not psychological integrationism) was sufficient to meet the deepest needs of man.
Then we had to prove that the ministry was not a personality cult but
that others from all walks of life and in various cultures and languages could learn to apply the same approach to resolving life problems and see it honored by the Spirit of God.

Having accomplished this, Grace Fellowship International is now
turning its attention to getting out the message of the Cross and re-
vival through missionary endeavors in various parts of the world.
The international offices are having a significant impact, but there is
a need for many more in this country who will go to various countries to introduce this proven approach to communicating the truth
of our identification with Christ.

Much of this can be done by volunteers who can take a short-term
missions trip to share with a believer who already understands the
message how to communicate it on a one-to-one basis. Those who
are not able to go to a foreign country can work with us to extend the
message of the Cross to other communities and states. We are particularly interested in networking with pastors who share the same
burden.

The network of believers who have read previous printings of this
book forms a pool from which to send volunteer missionaries literally
to the four corners of the earth. Pray with us that many will be chal-
lenged to become short-term volunteer missionaries to strengthen
the body of Christ in this country and around the world.

This book goes out with the prayer that many will see its message
as appropriate, if not for their own needs, for many of their friends
and families. Many have found victory. Some have even returned
from the brink of suicide as the Holy Spirit used the simple presenta-
tion of our resources in Christ to meet them at their extremity. May
he meet you at your point of need in life and ministry.

Dr. Charles Solomon
1999

Introduction

Spirituotherapy is a word coined by Dr. Solomon to identify an approach to counseling (spiritual ministry) that makes the believer's relationship to the cross of Christ central to its method and goal. He was called of God in 1967 through Isaiah 58:10-12 to found and pioneer the approach as a result of God's work in his life in 1965. In recent years it has also come to be known as "exchanged-life counseling." In Spirituotherapy, the Holy Spirit is the Therapist who renews the mind and transforms the life in accordance with Romans 12:2. Spirituotherapy (exchanged-life counseling) was developed by Dr. Solomon at Grace Fellowship International (GFI), which was established in Denver, Colorado, in 1969 as a nonprofit, tax-exempt corporation and has now been relocated to Pigeon Forge, Tennessee. GFI is nondenominational, and its allegiance is to the Lord Jesus Christ and to the infallible and immutable Word of God.

Dr. Solomon, founder and president of GFI, received his B.S. degree from East Tennessee State University and his Master of Personnel Service degree from the University of Colorado. He began counseling part-time while employed with Martin-Marietta Corporation (now Lockheed-Martin), where he worked as an engineer and in contracts from 1951 until 1970 after completing his undergraduate work in 1951. This counseling was under a contract with the Department of Labor, by which Martin-Marietta was to hire and train "hard-core unemployed" females for clerical work. His master's thesis was based on the results of that program.

He earned a Doctor of Education degree from the University of

Northern Colorado in 1972. Much of the work toward this degree was in original research, counseling, writing, and teaching associated with the new discipline of Spirituotherapy, which the state of Colorado formally recognized by awarding a doctorate. The remainder was in counseling and psychology. The first edition of this book was his project in lieu of a doctoral dissertation.

The first GFI office opened on February 1, 1970, in Denver, Colorado. The first branch office opened in 1975, and the first international office was opened in Argentina in January 1981. Thousands of people from six continents and many countries have received some type of training, which began with the first seminar in Colorado Springs in 1972. Contributions to GFI are tax deductible, and only those sent to the corporate headquarters in Tennessee will support the pioneering work of Dr. Solomon. No part of contributions sent to other organizations and/or addresses will find their way to Dr. Solomon's ministry.

Contributions and inquiries about the mission of GFI may be addressed to

Grace Fellowship International
P.O. Box 368
Pigeon Forge, TN 37868
Web site: www.SolomoNet.org

ONE

Experiencing
the Cross of Christ

Knowing what the world is like today, I feel certain that you or some of those you love are facing problems that are impossible to resolve or even to face in the strength of human resources. Some time ago a pastor friend shared his belief that many pastors today are experiencing severe pressure in their ministries. He spoke of problems in the pastors' own lives and families and of conflicts within the life of the church. He further stated that this has not always been the case.

Loyalty to the local church seems to be at an all-time low, which is to be expected as a logical result of the breakdown of family structures. This, along with the usual problems faced by pastors, puts them in a rather unenviable position.

I understand what my pastor friend was talking about, because part of my past experience in dealing with just such pressure, I believe, has helped me find some answers. I believe that in dealing with these pressures, it is vital to have an understanding of some of the concepts relating to rejection and identity. And though not everyone has the help of a counselor, we all have access to the infallible Word of God and *the Counselor,* the Holy Spirit, who alone is able to transform our lives by the renewing of our minds, as the apostle Paul promised in Romans 12:2.

I was one of those who did not have the opportunity to share my needs with another believer who could point me to answers from the Scriptures, either about the meaning of salvation or for advice about the rest of my spiritual journey. Although I had trusted Christ as a

1

seventeen-year-old, I entered the kingdom still carrying a load of emotional problems that hindered my effectiveness in facing normal activities, to say nothing of the stresses of life.

I grew up with more than my share of inferiority feelings as well as an ability to hide those feelings from others. Academically, I enjoyed my school years but was uncomfortable socially. Even though I had somewhat better than average intelligence, I felt I would fail at the mundane pursuits of life. My high school years were very unhappy, and I viewed graduation as an escape from an intolerable existence.

I was determined to get through college, even though I felt that I would flunk out. I studied fairly hard the first quarter and made straight A's and the dean's list. Even so, it did not change the way I *felt*. I *knew* I would find some way to make above-average grades, while still *feeling* that everyone in the class knew more than I did. During my childhood, circumstances had progammed my mind to go one way and my emotions another.

In my second year of college, I met my wife and right away tried to convince her of how inferior I was. However, she saw my above-average academic performance and found it difficult to believe that I was as inferior as I presented myself to be. We were married between my junior and senior years, and she taught school while I completed my last year. I had begun a preengineering major, since I found it unthinkable to consider a career that involved public speaking. Stage fright had severely limited my options. I finally majored in mathematics and got a teaching credential, even though I didn't want to teach. Eventually I was hired by what is now Lockheed Martin Corporation in Baltimore, Maryland, and I set out trying to behave like an engineer. I felt inferior in the profession for which I had prepared, so you can imagine how I felt in one for which I had little preparation.

Our three children were born by the time I was twenty-six. This period, my twenties, was a time of inner conflict. I suffered from severe depression and anxiety and had an ulcer by the time I was twenty-five. At one point I was taking four hundred milligrams of Thorazine a day. At the age of twenty-seven, I sold out completely to the Lord Jesus Christ, but I did not know where to go from there. I got involved in the church and worked very hard, but I found that working for the Lord did not necessarily produce spiritual growth. I accepted a transfer to Denver with the corporation, where we became involved in a solid, Bible-believing church, and I continued the ceaseless rounds of compulsive service. My work and family responsibilities increased, but increasing depression and anxiety diminished my capacity to produce. Obviously, my employment and continuous work for the church in my off hours took up most of the time I should have had for my family. This, along with the severe emotional problems, did little to commend me as a husband and father.

When I could get my mind off myself and become involved in some activity, I enjoyed myself to some degree, but my unresolved inner conflict was always just beneath the surface. At age thirty-four, I was tentatively diagnosed as having multiple sclerosis. While that diagnosis was never confirmed, privately I was disappointed that it was not cancer. Dying with cancer would have provided what I would have considered an honorable discharge from life.

Depression and anxiety reached their peak in October 1965, when I was thirty-five. At times I wept all the way home from work. I felt boxed in, with no escape. I would hold to this or that promise from God, hoping that I might find an answer to my plight.

On the night of October 25, I knew that I could not go on one more day. I was on medication for pain in the back of my head, and had I not been a Christian, suicide would have been the only option.

It was at that point that the Spirit of God intervened in my life. Late that night I was reading Galatians 2:20: "I am crucified with Christ." I had given up hope of finding help from God or anyone else. But God graciously and sovereignly moved in my life that night and released me from all the anxiety, depression, pain in the back of my head, and inferiority feelings of a lifetime.

This feeling of total freedom lasted a day or two. Then some of the old feelings settled back in, and I had to learn a process the Bible calls "walking in the Spirit." Beyond the first step of being "filled with the Spirit," I had to learn to continue the process of allowing the Holy Spirit to have control of my life.

Since I had no one to disciple me in this new way of life, the next couple of years I was up and down spiritually. During the first year, I read as many as a hundred books, including biographies and autobiographies, on the subject of the abundant life. I also spent many hours studying Paul's epistles to gain a theological understanding of what God had done in my life.

After two years' time, it occurred to me that if God could set *me* free from my emotional disturbances, he could do the same for others. It seemed that the field of counseling would give me the means to share some of the answers I had found. So I enrolled in a master's program in counseling at the University of Colorado, although its counseling program, as you might expect, was not noted for its spiritual content.

As I was praying about this decision to enter the counseling ministry, the Lord gave me two verses from Isaiah:

> If thou draw out thy soul to the hungry, and satisfy the afflicted soul; then shall thy light rise in obscurity, and thy darkness be as the noonday: and the Lord shall guide thee continually, and satisfy thy soul in drought, and make fat thy bones: and thou shalt be like a watered garden, and like a spring of water, whose waters fail not. (Isa. 58:10-11)

I completed the master's program in December 1969, and God sovereignly provided a layoff from my position in the aerospace industry the following January. In February 1970 I began a counseling ministry and at the same time began a doctoral program at the University of Northern Colorado, where I was allowed to design an innovative program that would integrate the spiritual and psychological dimensions of man. My study program would lead to a doctor of education in *Spirituotherapy,* as I chose to call it.

I found atheists, agnostics, and Jewish professors to be more helpful to me than some Christians, who would try to force me into a system that omitted or deemphasized the effect that our relationship to the cross of Christ is to have on our lives. Even today some Christians oppose these teachings, and I am trying to learn not to be defensive.

The cross of Christ, however, has never been a place where many people gather for fellowship, nor will it ever be. Those who have embraced the Cross and its teachings don't think of themselves as having "arrived," except at the bottom. The Cross in the life of the believer involves brokenness and suffering, just as it did for our Lord. Since pastors, counselors, psychologists, and psychiatrists are people, just like the rest of us, their road to victory over the flesh must be the same as ours.

There is no such thing as an "end run" around the Cross. None of us is greater than his Master, and all must go the way of the Cross if we are to have victory in our Christian experience. Until believers understand this, they will continue to resist the message that life must come out of death and victory out of defeat, whether in counseling or in any other kind of ministry.

What I learned during those days in 1965 was that the experience of the Cross is an ongoing process. God allowed many things to come into my life, during those days and since, to contribute to my spiritual growth. I learned that we are all in the process of *becoming* in experience who we *already are* in Christ by position. Until we are one day with him, we will have to continue dealing with sin, in the world and in ourselves.

Rejection and Its Effects

As with all approaches to counseling, there has been continuing development over the years. When I began counseling in 1970, I routinely took a life history of the counselee as part of the intake interview. As I did so, I discovered a common thread running through the lives of those with whom I worked: *rejection.* Some clients had been overtly rejected, verbally or physically, by their parents or by some other significant person in their lives. Others were rejected in more subtle ways.

Those who have been openly rejected by their parents may understand to some degree the resulting anger and distrust. However, often these people did not see the connection between their present emotional and social maladjustment and the traumatic events of their childhoods.

Those who have been rejected in subtle ways may have just as much emotional damage but be unaware of the source. Some actually heard their parents say that the children were not wanted (overt rejection), while in other cases, parents of infants gave them up for adoption. Adopted people, for instance, have by definition been rejected. Although the natural parents may have had no other choice, adopted children often think there was (and is) something wrong with them that caused the rejection. Others were rejected but didn't recognize it as rejection at the time.

By *rejection* I mean "the absence of meaningful love." Being rejected does not mean there is no love involved but that, for one reason or another, it is not fulfilling or edifying love. *The result of rejection is usually the impaired ability to give and receive love.*

People feel rejection for many reasons, such as overprotection, performance-based acceptance, the premature death of their parents, an extended hospitalization in infancy, and even the realization that they are the opposite sex from what the parents wanted. Sometimes the rejection is subtle, unintentional, unrecognized, unavoidable, or even all of the above.

The *overprotected child* is not allowed to make decisions appropriate to his own age, so he doesn't develop confidence in himself or in his decision-making ability. His parents are telling him, by default, that he is not capable of making decisions. And, deeming himself to be inferior, he develops an inferiority complex. His parents love him so much that they do everything for him except allow him to become a person! Obviously this is unintentional, and usually neither the parents nor the child realize what is happening.

The overprotected (spoiled) child often becomes ambivalent toward his parents. He loves them for what they do *for* him but resents them for what they do *to* him. Since he usually isn't aware of what they did to him, he feels and thinks that he resents them for no cause, and then he feels guilty because of his feelings of resentment and his lack of appreciation. An only child is more likely to be overprotected than one from a family of several children.

The child whose parents love him for what he *does* rather than for what he *is* (performance-based acceptance) also feels rejected. His good performance is accepted, but his person may be rejected.

One who loses his parents through death or divorce, prior to his conscious memory, experiences a perceived or felt rejection but may never understand it. In a similar manner, an infant who is in an incubator for an extended period of time may experience a withdrawal of love through no fault of the parents but merely from medical necessity. However, it may leave emotional scars on the child.

One woman with whom I spoke had spent the first three months of her life in an incubator. She could not accept the fact that her parents loved her at all until she was twenty-three years old. Obviously, while she was in the incubator she was not lying there thinking that her parents hated her, but the void that was built into her emotions during that time in the incubator prevented her from *receiving* her parents' love, which was there in abundance. She received love but *perceived* or felt rejection.

An infant loses a primary source of love and acceptance if his parents are taken away through death. And, though it was no one's fault, the effects on interpersonal relationships can carry over into adulthood. Since the child has lost a trusted parent, in adulthood he or she may find it hard to trust anyone. One fourteen-year-old boy, whose father and brother were killed in an auto accident and whose mother was seriously injured when the boy was six, was unable to attend school and studied under a teacher who came to his home. When I talked to him about surrendering everything to Christ, he grabbed his abdomen as if I had stabbed him with a knife. He asked, "Do you have an antacid?" He said he had been holding himself together and holding in his feelings for nine years and couldn't let go.

A person who suffers from rejection will often reject himself in some facet of his personality, sometimes in a socially acceptable way and sometimes not, especially when he tries to compensate for the unhealthy emotions that plague him. The effects of rejection on the personality vary, depending on the severity and duration of the rejection and the age of the person when it occurs. Sometimes a loving grandparent or another special person can lessen the effects of the rejection in a child's life.

A rejected person will reject not only himself but also others, even marriage partners. Such a person also tends to blame others for problems in the relationship, absolving himself or herself from responsibility.

Some rejected people have trouble accepting and discharging responsibilities. Such a person would rather not try something than to try and fail, since the failure will cause him to feel even worse about himself. One such man, a chemical engineer who was doing a creditable job, felt himself a failure as a person and an employee. One day his supervisor came to him and said, "We are going to give you a five-thousand-dollar-a-year increase in salary and an automobile." John replied, "That does it! I quit!" He turned on his heel and walked out of the office. His internal conflicts were so severe that he felt he couldn't possibly accept any further responsibility.

The cause and effects of rejection are covered more fully in my books *The Ins and Out of Rejection* and *The Rejection Syndrome and the Way to Acceptance*.

The answer to rejection is *acceptance*. Human acceptance, however, will not heal the damaged emotions after rejection has done its dirty work. It does help, and often it will be the only help available, but the experience of being accepted in Christ is the only true curative.

Identity

The importance of *identity* and the many ways it affects the whole of our existence has also become a part of my counseling. It is important because what a person sees as his identity, or the identity he would *like* to make work for him, will determine where he looks for acceptance. See chapter 6, pages 90 and 91, for diagrams on identity.

Most believers live with an identity that has been assigned to them—either positive or negative, depending on the extent of rejection—or with an identity they have built for themselves. Many are so-called self-made men and women and end up being dissatisfied with the job they have done. Usually the identity has been based on things, money, people, power, and accomplishments, or lack of them. Identity based on temporal things will naturally be subject to change without notice.

The apostle Paul differentiates between our fleshly identity and our spiritual identity, that is, what we are as a result of human resources and what we are through the Holy Spirit's power. Again, as with the problem of rejection, the cure for an unacceptable fleshly identity is a true spiritual identity, which only a proper relationship to Christ can give us.

In the flesh, our natural resources, we have been programmed in certain directions by the teaching and experiences we have had. Some people are programmed so that their identity is fulfilled through accumulation of money and things; others are programmed toward success in business or some other achievements. Some are programmed toward sensuality, and some even toward religious pursuits.

For the believer, all of these are false and unsatisfactory identities, since our true identity is based on who we are in Christ. Many believers, however, never seem to discover their true identity until they get to Glory. David Needham deals with this vital truth in his book *Birthright* (Multnomah, 1982). The problem is that many people are living out of the wrong identity—the one shaped by being "conformed to this world" rather than by being "transformed by the renewing of [their] minds" (Rom. 12:2).

The answer to the problem, though many have called such a suggestion "overly simplistic," lies in exchanging the identity that is based on our personal history and the influence of indwelling sin, for our perfect identity in Christ. Such a transaction truly takes a miracle, but it is the kind of miracle in which the Holy Spirit majors. The Holy Spirit does not enter our lives to patch up our old identities but to put into effect our true identity as redeemed children of the King of kings. Paul described this work within us:

> That the God of our Lord Jesus Christ, the Father of glory, may give unto you the spirit of wisdom and revelation in the knowledge of him: the eyes of your understanding being enlight-

ened; that ye may know what is the hope of his calling, and what the riches of the glory of his inheritance in the saints, and what is the exceeding greatness of his power to us-ward who believe, according to the working of his mighty power, which he wrought in Christ, when he raised him from the dead, and set him at his own right hand in the heavenly places. (Eph. 1:17-20)

The same power God used in raising Jesus from the dead is operative in us as we place our faith in what was accomplished through Christ's resurrection. Paul wrote, "If, when we were enemies, we were reconciled to God by the death of his Son, much more, being reconciled, we shall be saved by his life" (Rom. 5:10).

Our identity is based on who we are in Christ, and it is to be claimed by faith, not by works—ours or any other's. We shed the trappings of the past by exchanging our fleshly identity for the Christ-life, by exchanging a life of defeat for a life of victory. Jesus told his followers, "If any man will come after me, let him deny himself, and take up his cross daily, and follow me" (Luke 9:23). Many have a faulty notion of what "self" and "denying self" really mean. Some think that denying themselves some worldly pleasures will fulfill this command. Others think that "taking up the cross" is bearing some burden, such as caring for a severely handicapped child. Obviously, it is difficult to deny ourselves if we don't know what "self" is.

What does it mean to embrace our own old identity, the one we are to deny if we are to exchange it for our new identity in Christ? As an analogy, suppose that you or someone you know is fifteen years old, unmarried, and pregnant. Abortion is not an option, and the girl has made a firm decision to give the baby up for adoption. Would you recommend that a young woman in such a situation see the baby prior to relinquishing him or not? In either case, what would be the rationale for your recommendation?

It would be easier to have the baby and leave the hospital without having seen him and, thus, avoid the trauma of separation. Or would it? At the time, it would seem easier, but would the young woman have faced the reality of the situation? Did you ever try to give away something you never had? Without seeing the baby, there is a sense of unreality about the whole incident. Yes, the girl has carried the baby in the womb, but there is a difference between that and holding the baby and owning him. Once the young mother has held the baby and owned and loved him for a day or so and then given.him to the adoptive parents, the reality hits with full force. Then it is possible to go through the grief process, the separation anxiety, or whatever other names could be given to the traumatic loss the young mother experiences.

Each of us needs to ask the question "Have I owned my 'baby,' or is there still a sense of unreality about the identity out of which I live?" Each of us must define our identity and look at it squarely to understand what we must lose if we are to live out our true identity in the Lord Jesus Christ. We must "lose our baby," which has been in the formation stage for a lifetime, if we are to know the joy, the blessing, of our new identity as accepted and dearly loved children of God in Christ.

> Said Jesus unto his disciples, If any man will come after me, let him deny himself, and take up his cross, and follow me. For whosoever will save his life shall lose it: and whosoever will lose his life for my sake shall find it. (Matt. 16:24-25)

TWO

How Spirituotherapy Works

In order to understand ourselves, we need to have a clear conception of how we are made up and how we function. Our thoughts, feelings, and behaviors derive from an identity that we may not have recognized, and our motivation for present actions and reactions is a function of that identity. Or, to put it another way, the identity we have been assigned by others or the one that we have built for ourselves, positive or negative, will have a great influence on the decisions we make and the way we relate to others.

Since we are, at the core, spiritual beings, it behooves us to know what our spiritual identity is and the influence that Spirit-given knowledge can have on our psychological and social functioning. Over the years, it has proved extremely helpful to most of those whom I have counseled to understand the makeup or constituency of humanity, known in theological circles as biblical anthropology. Obviously, there are many views on this vital matter, but the discussions here will be limited to what the New Testament seems to support.

Two major Scripture references suggest that human beings are made up of three parts—body, soul, and spirit (the trichotomy view). Additional references also seem to support the assertion that we have a spirit that functions as a separate entity (1 Thess. 5:23; Heb. 4:12). We often view human beings as being material and immaterial. These two component parts are sometimes called body and soul, or body and mind (the dichotomy view). But this latter view does not allow for a spirit, even though it would teach that we function spiritually. Although in many ways humans function somewhat like members of the animal kingdom, albeit on a higher psychological level, I believe that it is the spirit that makes us intrinsically different from animals.

It is important to use a model that accords with Scripture when we try to explain psychological and spiritual functions and that we use biblical terminology rather than a purely psychological model. Otherwise, we come up with some vague generalities that will not support a true integration of psychology and theology. Paul wrote: "The very God of peace sanctify you wholly; and I pray God your whole spirit and soul and body be preserved blameless unto the coming of our Lord Jesus Christ" (1 Thess. 5:23). The writer of Hebrews wrote: "For the word of God is quick, and powerful, and sharper than any twoedged sword, piercing even to the dividing asunder of soul and spirit, and of the joints and marrow, and is a discerner of the thoughts and intents of the heart" (Heb. 4:12).

Other biblical references to the soul and spirit are not so definitive, but many allude to the existence of the soul and the spirit as separate entities. For example, when the Lord Jesus was on the cross, he, existing in a body, chose—an act of the soul—to dismiss his spirit. Paul wrote: "But he that is joined unto the Lord is one spirit" (1 Cor. 6:17). Obviously, this speaks of a union of the spirit as opposed to a union of the soul. Drawing on the language of Scripture, we might say that man *is* a spirit, that he *has* a soul, and that he *lives* in a body. *It is vital that this entire book be read with this understanding, since some statements cold be misconstrued if applied to any other than a trichotomous (tripartite) view of man.*

Since the prime concern of this book is to discover our true identity and to see a spiritual resolution for psychological and interpersonal symptoms, we need to see how the concept of identity relates to man. To do this, we need to begin with Adam, since that is where it all began! Adam had a perfect identity, and he found his entire meaning in his relationship with God. The following diagram shows his makeup of spirit, soul, and body. In Genesis we read that man

(Adam) was created in the image of God (1:26). He was created innocent and remained in this condition, able to communicate with God,
until the Fall. Though the spirit of Adam is not mentioned specifi-
cally, we read, "The Lord God formed man of the dust of the ground,
and breathed into his nostrils the breath of life [or lives], and man
became a living soul" (2:7).

DIAGRAM 1
ADAM PRIOR TO THE FALL

RELATES TO OTHERS — **SOUL** | **SPIRIT** → RELATES TO GOD

PERSONALITY   INNOCENT SPIRIT

BODY

RELATES TO ENVIRONMENT

The spirit at creation was not contaminated with sin, and Adam
functioned on a supernatural level in naming the animals and completing all the other tasks God gave him. The arrows (or arcs)
inside the circle in diagram 1 depict interaction and interrelation-
ships between spirit, soul, and body, with no conflict. The arrows
pointing toward the outside indicate interaction with God as well as
with other people and with the environment. These along with
other terms used or implied in the Scriptures are adequate to explain a person's totality and his intrapersonal and interpersonal
functions.

God told Adam, "Of the tree of the knowledge of good and evil, thou shalt not eat of it: for in the day that thou eatest thereof thou shalt surely die" (Gen. 2:17). Since Adam and Eve did eat (Gen. 3:6), we know that some kind of death took place that day. Obviously, it was not physical death. Their souls continued to function psychologically. As a result of their sin, physical death did eventually occur, but some other kind of death took place that day. It could only have been a spiritual death, and the remainder of the Bible addresses itself to the consequences of that event. Diagram 2 describes human beings after the Fall.

As you look at these diagrams, you will note that the *soul* might be called our self consciousness, or the personality through which we relate to others—actually our psychological makeup. The *spirit* is our God consciousness, or the facet of our makeup by which we relate to God. The *body,* of course, is the means by which, through our five senses, we relate to the world and our environment. In summary, we relate to others through our soul, to God through our spirit, and to our environment through our body. The soul is composed of mind (or intellect), the emotions (or affections), and the will (or volition). The *spirit* has similar functions, but it will not be helpful to discuss them at this point.

As depicted by the arrow between body and soul in diagram 2, physical problems such as an endocrine imbalance or other ailments can have an adverse effect on our emotional state. Likewise, we can suffer from long-standing psychological symptoms that affect our spiritual life and hamper our walk with God. Being spiritually maladjusted will produce or amplify existing psychological symptoms. So difficulties in one of the three areas may, in turn, have an adverse effect on another area. It will be necessary to refer constantly to the wheel diagram as we proceed to differentiate the functions of spirit, soul, and body and the understandings we should have regarding needs and problems in each area.

Of course, the first and prime consideration is our relationship with God. Unless and until there is a personal relationship, the content of this book is just so much rhetoric. That initial personal relationship and all that pertains to it have to do with the *spirit* and are explained in terms of our *salvation.*

DIAGRAM 2

MAN—A TRI-UNITY

As you will note in diagram 2, there is now a smaller circle in the center to depict the fact that man after the Fall was *flesh,* meaning that from that point on he lived a self-centered life. Later in Genesis we read, "The Lord said, My spirit shall not always strive with man, for . . . he also is flesh" (6:3).

Throughout this book, the words *flesh* and *self* will be used interchangeably when referring to the control center of a believer who is living out of his own resources. When the word *self* is used, it should not be understood as meaning the same as *personality,* for example.

In the center of the circle is the letter *S* (self), referring to the fact that Adam positionally became *flesh* or self-centered and that each of us is born into the world with the same dilemma (Rom. 5:12). Later we will see that this self-centered position is used of the believer as a *condition.* At the Fall, Adam's and Eve's identity shifted from God to themselves in relation to Satan. Their problem afterward was not so much the individual acts of sin they committed as the fact that they were now in an entirely different sphere of life, or death, as the case may be. Although they each had a functioning spirit, they now functioned toward Satan instead of toward God. We might say that the *spirit was dead to God and alive to Satan.*

The initial personal relationship and some of its outworkings are listed under "Spirit" in diagram 3 on page 24, and some are explained as follows:

Salvation

Variously defined as conversion to Christ, being born again, regeneration, being saved, trusting Christ as Savior and Lord, accepting Christ, and receiving Christ, salvation is entering into a personal relationship with God through personal faith in Jesus Christ. Unless the Lord Jesus Christ is *in* our life, obviously, he cannot make the necessary changes. His entrance into the life brings about a spiritual birth that is only the beginning of our life in Christ. Before we trust the Lord Jesus Christ in a personal surrender, the Holy Spirit must convince us that we are *born* sinners.

Paul concluded, "Wherefore, as by one man [Adam] sin entered into the world, and death by sin; and so death passed upon all men, for that all have sinned" (Rom. 5:12). Since we are born with a sinful nature, or "old man" (Rom. 6:6; Eph. 4:22), we naturally commit sins. Paul wrote: "All have sinned and come short of the glory of God" (Rom. 3:23).

The penalty for sin is stated: "The wages of sin is death; but the gift of God is eternal life through Jesus Christ our Lord" (Rom. 6:23). The death penalty must be paid, and it *has* been paid: "God commendeth [exhibits or proves] his love toward us, in that, while we were yet sinners, Christ died for us" (Rom. 5:8).

When we are ready to admit that we are ungodly and are ready to believe on the Lord Jesus Christ, then we will be justified and counted righteous in God's sight. "To him that worketh not, but believeth on him that justifieth the ungodly, his faith is counted for righteousness" (Rom. 4:5). The method is very simple. We merely believe what the Bible says about us (that we are ungodly sinners), and we also believe what the Bible says about the Lord Jesus (that he was and is God, that he died for our sins, and that he rose from the dead). This is very clearly stated in Scripture: "If thou shalt confess with thy mouth the Lord Jesus, and shalt believe in thine heart that God hath raised him from the dead, thou shalt be saved. For with the heart man believeth unto righteousness; and with the mouth confession is made unto salvation" (Rom. 10:9-10).

After we hear and believe, we must call upon God in prayer: "Whosoever shall call upon the name of the Lord shall be saved" (Rom. 10:13). A simple prayer will do, such as: "Dear God, I know I am a sinner. I believe that you sent your Son, the Lord Jesus Christ, to die for my sins, that he was buried, and that he rose from the dead. I surrender now and turn from a life of sin and trust the Lord Jesus Christ to forgive my sins and to be my life. Thank you for saving me, for Jesus' sake. Amen."

On the basis of God's infallible Word, he saves us when we believe and call upon him. After we have settled the question of salvation in our lives, we must learn to rejoice in the *assurance* that God has done what he said he would do.

Assurance

It is possible to be saved but not be assured of that salvation. Our assurance must be based on the facts of Scripture rather than on fluctuating feelings. The person who is sometimes labeled *neurotic* most often wants to feel something rather than to believe it, and his style of living is to distort reality. As a result, there is no reason for him to believe that his feelings will be trustworthy in the matter of salvation.

There is a profound difference between doubting one's salvation (mental) and feeling unsaved (emotional). Most people who lack assurance *feel* unsaved. However, most of us do not make a distinction between the functions of the mind and the emotions. Neither do most personal workers, who attempt to help those who lack assurance. In our attempts to help, we often appeal to someone's mind with the facts of the gospel when it's really the emotions that are the cause of the confusion. When the emotions are being controlled by lies the person has been believing, there is no way the emotions will ever agree with truth. Therefore, a person may *know* (mentally) that he is saved, and never doubt his salvation, and yet *feel* (emotionally) unsaved for a lifetime.

A veteran missionary who had felt unsaved off and on for more than a quarter century was greatly relieved when he finally saw this distinction. Although the feelings did not change immediately, having an understanding of the problem gave new light. The following day his testimony to a group of missionaries was, "Today I *know* I am saved, and I don't care whether I *feel* saved or not!"

The Bible, speaking to believers, tells us that we are to *know* that we have eternal life (1 John 5:13). It is not at all presumptuous to take God at his Word and simply rest in it. We can establish our assurance only by accepting God's Word for what it is. After we have assurance of our salvation, we can go on to find *security* in that fact.

Security

Our relationship with God is unbreakable—eternal. We are secure in that relationship, and we cannot have assurance if we are not secure and confident that this relationship is lasting. Paul wrote: "Your life is hid with Christ in God" (Col. 3:3). If we do not realize this, our assurance cannot be solid because we will be afraid of losing our salvation. And if we are afraid of losing it, we will struggle to do something in order to maintain it, such as good works. As a result, we cease to live trusting in God's grace and begin to live again trusting in our obedience to the law for our salvation. This Paul described as "falling from grace" (Gal. 5:4). Many evangelical Christians live this way—saved by grace but, in the practical outworking, still bound by the law.

Unless a person has his security nailed down, he is unlikely to mature in his relationship with Jesus Christ. Of course, assurance and security really go hand in hand. You cannot experience one to any great degree without the other.

Acceptance

Some accept the Lord Jesus Christ as personal Savior and Lord and then spend the rest of their lives trying to get him to accept them. Of course, this is a futile effort because the Scriptures assure us that "we are accepted in the beloved [Christ]" (Eph. 1:6). Our acceptance by Christ doesn't depend on our good works or on how much we read the Bible or on how much we go to church or on any other effort we may expend. Our acceptance is rooted solely in his finished work at Calvary—not in our work *for* him. Salvation is by grace from start to finish. Acceptance is by grace too. God accepts his Son, and since we are in his Son, "accepted in the beloved," he accepts us as well.

Many today have difficulty believing that their parents or their peers accept them. In fact, many people feel that no one really accepts them. As a result, they come to feel that God relates to them in the same manner. If they are not fit for other people to accept, why should God accept them? Of course, this isn't the case. But if they *feel* that way, that perception can govern their behavior.

Then what is the answer? We must come to the place where, through the illumination of the Holy Spirit, we realize that we are accepted. We *are* acceptable, not because of anything we have done, but because of the great things the Lord Jesus Christ has done. When we were saved—when we trusted Christ as our personal Savior and Lord—we were put *into* Christ (1 Cor. 1:30). Having been put into Christ, we are accepted by God *in Christ.* In this, as in the initial salvation experience, we must take God at his word and believe what he says regardless of how we may feel about it. As we do that, our feelings begin to line up with the facts.

Acceptance by God and identification with Christ in his death, burial, and resurrection are much like opposite sides of a coin. When someone experiences one, he will realize the other also. A case in point is that of a woman who had been filled with extreme hostility. She had tried psychiatric treatment before coming to our Grace Fellowship office. After she had approximately three counseling interviews and attended three lectures I gave, God set her free. She had intellectually understood the principles set forth in this book when, on Saturday night, she began to meditate on Galatians 2:20: "I am crucified with Christ." On Sunday morning as she was driving to church, she was singing the hymn "Calvary Love." As she sang the refrain "I long to be worthy of Calvary love," the Holy Spirit dealt with her. She realized that *in Christ she was worthy.* She began to weep and cry out, "I am accepted. I am acceptable!" The question of her acceptance was settled, as was the extreme hostility. No longer was she dominated by psychological difficulties that had beset her since childhood.

Total Commitment

Salvation, assurance, security, and acceptance leave us still lacking in one important point—total commitment. We use terms such as *consecration, dedication, surrender, submission,* and others to denote this vital step in the Christian's life, but it is necessary to define the term as we will be using it throughout this book.

Paul wrote: "I beseech you therefore, brethren, by the mercies of God, that ye present your bodies a living sacrifice, holy, acceptable unto God, which is your reasonable service" (Rom. 12:1). Total commitment, according to this verse, is something *we* can do. It is our "reasonable service." It is an act of the will by which we tell our Father than we want more than anything else in this world to have his will accomplished in our lives, whatever that means. We may not know his specific purpose for our life, but after we have wholly committed our lives to him, he begins to bring it to pass (Ps. 37:5).

Total surrender is essential to total usefulness. Occasionally a person accepts the Lord Jesus Christ as Savior and makes him Lord of his life at the beginning. This is what should happen in all conversions. One should not accept Jesus Christ as Savior and then wait ten or fifteen years to yield completely to him. This should take place the day a person accepts Christ. When it doesn't, a person has to see the futility of running his own life—or ruining it, as is frequently the case—and come to the place where he is ready to say, "Lord, I want to take my hands off my life. I want you to run it."

This decision is comparable to the ceremony in which a man and woman are joined in marriage. Each of them says, by an act of the will, "I do." Based on this act of their wills, before God and a minister, they are pronounced man and wife. They have met the legal requirements for marriage. The act of the will has been made, but they are still not man and wife until the marriage union is consummated. With an act of the will they have made a decision that changes the entire course of their lives. But neither of them feels automatically like a wife or a husband. The total commitment to the Lord is much the same, in which, by an act of our will, we say "I do" or "I will." "Whatever you want, Lord. Your will be done in my life."

Our wills have been exercised, but usually our lives are not miraculously transformed at that time, although some persons' are. A few who come for counseling are at the point where there is no way out. When they come through in a complete surrender, God consummates the transformation in the life immediately or in a very short time. But in many cases, once this surrender is made, with or without emotion, there is little observable change. From that point, the responsibility is turned over to God, and he begins to bring about a consummation of his purpose and plan in their lives.

Looking back to Romans 12:1, we surrender our lives as a "living sacrifice." This hearkens back to the Old Testament sacrifice, which was a lamb placed on the altar. The lamb had no choice. Someone else put him there. As he was bound on the altar, he was totally committed by someone else to be the sacrifice. He could not say to the priest, "Now, listen, do anything to me, but don't cut my throat!" That was *exactly* what the priests had in mind. The lamb was totally under the control of another.

But this is exactly what our surrender must be if our faithful High Priest is to bring about the consummation in our lives, by which we will experience the fullness of our union with Jesus Christ. Unlike the lamb, we have control, but we relinquish it, submitting ourselves to be placed on the altar.

DIAGRAM 3

In the salvation experience referred to earlier, on our invitation Christ enters into our spirit. This is represented by the *C* in the lower part of diagram 3. Christ is in the life, but he can be in the life without being in the *center* of the life. Tragically, this is true of a great many Christians. In fact, that person may be so busy with life that Christ might remain on the periphery. Another person may be so busy working *for* the Lord that he doesn't have time to spend *with* him. As a result, Christ is not central in the life. But because of the trials and adversities that God permits in our lives, we may realize that we need Christ in the center of our lives—not off on the periphery somewhere. If Christ is not at the center, someone or something else is. The thing or person that is so important that it becomes the motivating force of our lives is referred to as the *center* of our life.

The *S* in the center of the circle might, for instance, represent *some thing,* such as a home or a cat or some other thing that we feel would really make us happy. Usually we strive and struggle to get these things, and once the newness wears off, we find we have won a hollow victory.

The center might be occupied by *some person*—a father, a mother, a husband, a wife, a child, a boyfriend, or a girlfriend—some person in our lives we seek to please or satisfy, or to satisfy us, so that we can feel good about ourselves. This might have either a positive or a negative orientation. For instance, one or both of our parents could cause us to feel a certain way about ourselves. Even though they might be hundreds of miles away or deceased, we still feel about ourselves the way they caused us to feel.

The *S* in the center might be *success,* however we choose to define it in our lives. A businessman could be struggling to get to the top, to become the president of the company. A minister may seek success by struggling to work, work, work to get to a place where he can have a more influential ministry or a larger church. Success for a student might be making all A's. Regardless of how people choose it, the motivating force in some lives is success.

For a sex deviate, *sex* might be the most important thing in life, in that his whole life is centered around it. For someone else it might be *drugs* and the experience to be derived from them. Heroin addicts might consider getting another fix the most important thing in life, so that becomes their all-consuming passion. For some, especially in the materialistic American culture, the most important thing is *money* and the things money can buy. But all of these manifestations represent things *we* want or something that we think will give *us* satisfaction. All of these *S* elements may be summed up in the term *self* (or flesh). (As I mentioned earlier, *self* as it is used in this book is not synonymous with *personality.* One renowned Christian psychologist erroneously claimed that I teach the annihilation of the personality—thus the reason for this disclaimer.)

Someone has said that we can drop the *h* from the word *flesh,* spell it backwards, and have the word *self.* It is correct to use the word *self* as a synonym for the *soul*—the mind, emotions, and will—that which constitutes us as unique individuals. The soul, in and of itself, is neutral. Whatever is placed in the center, *S* or *C,* becomes the driving force that empowers the soul, determining its attitudes and actions and the ultimate worth of that which results. Self in the center of the life means *we* are in control or, at least, are trying to be. Of course, no one is able by himself to control his own life. The prophet Jeremiah says, "It is not in man that walketh to direct his steps" (Jer. 10:23). We are designed so that if we will give our volitional consent, God will control our spirit, our spirit will then control our soul, and our soul will control our body. This is God's plan; and for it to work, Christ must be at the control center. We should be Christ centered rather than self-centered. But many Christians, even those in full-time Christian work, find that they are still doing it for Christ rather than his doing it through them.

Hudson Taylor was an example of this. As a young man, he was saved and called into the ministry. After receiving his theological and medical training, he went to the mission field and was used of God to found the China Inland Mission (now Overseas Missionary Fellowship). He went out completely in faith, totally dependent on God to supply every need, financial and otherwise. God blessed Hudson Taylor's work and sent out many more missionaries who also had to be completely dependent on God. But Taylor was on the mission field between ten and fifteen years before he finally came to the end of Hudson Taylor and all his own resources and quit trying to work *for* God. Then Christ began to live and work *through* him.

God does not want us to work *for* him, to witness *for* him, to live *for* him. He wants to get *self* out of the way so he can work through us. This is the lesson that many Christians never learn. Usually, it is learned only through hardship, trial, affliction, and suffering, until we come to the point where we deal with self. Then self is no longer the center of our life. Our minds and emotions are controlled by the indwelling Christ as we will or reckon upon our resources in him. Until this process is completed, self is in control, and we use our own wills and minds to run our lives instead of using them only in the *doing* role. In other words, we are *doing* in order to *be* rather than *being* in order to *do*. As a result, our lives are less effective. If God is running our lives, then our minds, emotions, and wills are free to serve his purposes unhampered by the additional duties of trying to decide how we should live our lives. As long as self is in control, the functions of the soul will operate in direct correspondence to the historical events that have characterized our maturation, and these may be worsened by the ways we have attempted to meet our own needs.

Soul

Looking now at the psychological, or "soul," functions, we will consider some needs and difficulties a person may face.

DIAGRAM 4

First of all, let us consider the often used term *inferiority,* a feeling that plagues most of us in some areas of our lives. Some people's feelings of inferiority are so intense that they hamper personal relationships. These feelings can hinder their work to such a degree that when they receive an assignment, they have to fight just to get to the place where they can finally begin the task. Once they get started, they usually do an exceptional job, but they still *feel* they cannot achieve. Their minds tell them one thing, and their feelings tell them another. Usually, they know intellectually that they are not inferior, but they feel that they are. Such a conflict can lead to serious emotional problems, as it did for me, because of the methods a person uses to compensate for it.

Feelings of *insecurity* present another problem. Some people are filled with fears and doubts about themselves and about what is going to happen next. Such people often must contend with the feeling that something terrible is going to happen to them. They cannot relax and have those good feelings inside because of their apprehensions, which, in turn, spawn other symptoms. Insecurity in the marriage relationship can give rise to jealousy, and jealousy to accusations, and the cycle often goes on until divorce results. Insecurity in the work relationship causes people to fear a demotion or the loss of a job, which causes workers to be ineffective and brings about the very results they feared. One pastor's wife was so jealous that the pastor couldn't have even an eighty-year-old secretary—not because of any indiscretions on his part but solely because of his wife's insecurity.

Feelings of *inadequacy,* another common problem, can take two forms—feelings of personal inadequacy or feelings of inadequacy in certain situations. Feelings of personal inadequacy, like feelings of inferiority, make people believe, in almost any situation, that they are incapable of coping with life. Others feel inadequate only in certain situations. For instance, a person might feel inadequate in his family role at home, but he might feel totally adequate on the job. He might be a professional man or an executive in a company, and his work is held in high esteem. He is admired, so he feels wonderful and stays overtime, possibly working ten or twelve hours a day. In the home relationship, he cannot get along with his wife or his children, so he stays at work and becomes a loyal company man. It is not necessarily because he likes the work so much but because he cannot make it at home. The converse could be true where a person who feels protected and safe at home has struggles with fear in his employment because he is really not making a success of it.

A fourth bad feeling is *guilt,* and again there are two forms of it. The first is *real guilt,* and we must face it as such. We must not try to explain it away or cover it and call it "guilt feelings" but must show it to be the result of sin, just as the Word of God proclaims it to be. The only cure for real guilt and its cause, sin, is forgiveness and cleansing through the blood of Jesus Christ. John wrote: "If we confess our sins, he is faithful and just to forgive us our sins, and to cleanse us from all unrighteousness" (1 John 1:9). This is the only way real guilt can be put away. Of course, all sin and guilt are dealt with when we are saved, when we trust Jesus Christ. But afterward, the sin that crops up in our lives must be dealt with by acknowledging it to God and forsaking it. If we do this, he forgives and cleanses us, as he promised in 1 John 1:9.

Apart from the real guilt that all of us have, from time to time many suffer from *imaginary guilt,* which feels exactly the same as real guilt. We can confess and confess and confess and still be plagued with the problem. Many who have these feelings think that they have committed the unpardonable sin or that there is some sin that they just cannot uncover. They do not know what it is, but they think that if they could just find it and confess it, they would be free.

Imaginary guilt may spring from a lack of love and acceptance. As an unwanted child, a person may feel no deep sense of belonging. Sometimes a child has been told that he is unwanted, while another merely senses it. As a result, the person becomes conscience stricken for just being there, feeling he is the cause of all the problems around him. If he were out of the picture, he thinks, the family would be fine. He feels guilty for even being a person.

Such imagined guilt can persist throughout life. Understanding the problem is the first step in turning it over to the Lord. Experiencing God's acceptance is the antidote to feelings of rejection.

We must consider also the general category of *worries, doubts, and fears.* When we have inner turmoil, we are prone to worry. God's Word admonishes us to "be anxious for nothing" (Phil. 4:6), but many don't know how to appropriate this truth, and they continue to worry about everything. When they do, they have various doubts—doubts that other people love them or doubts that God is real. They may doubt that he will meet their needs, and they begin to fret. Nagging doubts cause many kinds of fears, the fear of failure or a myriad other forms. Fear is all-pervasive, and it can really wreck us. It can become an irrational fear, a phobia. The underlying cause is a faulty faith. In fact, all five of the preceding symptoms are indicative of a failure to trust in Christ and depend upon him fully.

There are people whose fears seem to have fears! The more the fears are compounded, the less space a person has in which to live. This may result in the inability to drive a car. Fear of people and crowds, *agoraphobia,* may cause some people to pull down the shades and become prisoners in their own homes.

When we have all these things going on inside and acting upon each other, inner turmoil results. The internal frustration is compounded by external stresses from family, work, and other adverse conditions. You will note on the wheel in diagram 4 that we have encircled all five items and labeled the result as frustration. Such frustration has a direct bearing on *self.* The result can be illustrated by the striking of a golf ball. If the ball has a live center, it will react with the club head and travel a great distance. If the center is dead, not much is going to happen. If self is very much alive and the frustration comes in, the result may be hostility. Such an agitated person can strike something with his hand or want to throw something.

The problem arises in dealing with these feelings of hostility. The prime goal of some psychotherapists is to teach such a person how to handle his hostility, a futile effort because as soon as the person learns how to handle it in one form, the problem is going to pop up in another form. The problem is not in knowing how to handle the hostility but knowing how to prevent it. Sometimes the hostility is projected onto someone else (displaced hostility), usually a person who does not deserve it. Acting out the hostility relieves the pressure to some extent, but that incurs additional guilt, which serves to increase the frustration, and then another hostile act is committed. On and on the cycle goes.

One form of psychotherapy advocates letting out the feelings—emotional catharsis—as a means of venting hostility. This is workable in the therapeutic climate, but not everyone has a safe situation in which to dump their hostility. Society at large does not accept negative feelings with tender loving care. Many people who are filled with hostility have no acceptable means of dealing with it. They cannot verbalize it satisfactorily, and they cannot exercise violence toward other people to get it out. They keep all or some of it inside. When hostility is kept inside, the conflict can travel in either of two directions, as shown in the diagram 5. It can affect our minds, our emotions, or both. If it influences the mind, several things can happen.

DIAGRAM 5

One is *fantasy.* A person can spend his time thinking how he would *like* things to be. A little of this is acceptable because sometimes we do make our daydreams come true. But if we live in a fantasy world, we are not effective in the real world. A person who is prone to this (and some who are not) might have a psychotic break and become *schizophrenic,* living in an unreal world. Such a person may have to be institutionalized and permitted to live in that unreal world because he is incapable of living in reality.

The person might become *paranoid* because of feelings of inadequacy or guilt. A person who feels inadequate usually blames his failures on someone else. This becomes a pattern, and he begins to believe his own lie. Eventually, he becomes certain that a person or group is really out to get him. This may also stem from guilt, the person feeling as if he should be punished. In his fantasy he imagines that someone intends him bodily harm. Instead of being completely out of touch with reality, he usually has well-structured delusions, while in other areas of life he may be in touch with reality.

The person may also become *obsessed* with certain thoughts of which he cannot rid himself. This problem sometimes results in obsessive-compulsive behaviors, such as hand washing, to get some kind of relief from the anxiety. A good definition of obsessive thoughts is that a person's mind is putting on a sideshow to keep it off the main event. Eventually, this sideshow may be more troublesome than the problem it was intended to replace.

These aberrations are not necessarily mental illness, but they are mental symptoms of a deeper problem—self at the center of the life. Treating symptoms rarely effects a permanent cure. People can go to psychiatrists much or all of their lives for treatment of such symptoms. Some chronic schizophrenics *do* have a problem with their brain chemistry. But I contend that many of those who are diagnosed as schizophrenic are denying reality to protect themselves from situations, external or internal, that they cannot face.

In addition to symptoms in the mind, the frustration can affect the emotions, another area of the soul. Or both the mind and emotions may be affected. A common effect on the emotions is *depression*. Hostility kept inward becomes depression. We push against ourselves. We take it out on ourselves instead of taking it out on someone else. We beat ourselves severely about the head and shoulders, which causes us to be depressed, anxious, and tied up in knots. A more homespun definition of depression is that of an internal temper tantrum. This can be simple depression, or it can become more severe and be termed reactive depression or clinical depression. Still these are not, at their root, mental problems or real emotional problems. They are symptoms of a deeper problem. The problem is usually treated by attempting to rid the afflicted one of the anxiety and depression that has been bottled up inside.

This anxiety and depression are usually contained until it is no longer possible to restrict it to the domain of the soul. Then it manifests itself in the body as a psychosomatic or psychophysiological symptom. Examples of these might be a tension headache that becomes a migraine or a nervous stomach and the need for ubiquitous antacid pills or a combination of antacids and tranquilizers. The nervous stomach is the breeding place for a peptic ulcer. Some other common ailments stemming from psychological conflict are hives, some forms of arthritis, asthma, skin rashes, spastic colon, heart palpitations, and respiratory ailments. It should be noted, however, that many of these ailments listed may also be true physiological problems that have nothing to do with psychological conflict. Physicians who have written on this subject estimate that approximately 60 to 80 percent of their patients have ailments caused by psychological conflict. If a person has "the peace of God which passeth all understanding" (Phil. 4:7), he cannot continue to have unabated emotional conflict. Ultimately, these physical or psychosomatic symptoms are spiritual problems; since the only complete answer is spiritual, the problem must be spiritual as well.

To summarize, it is because *self* is at the center of the life that all of this conflict develops and continues to grow. The problems may have been there since childhood, but the fact that they continue means that *self* is running the life. It may be a good self; it may be a bad self; it may be in between; but it is still self, and *self in control of the life is repugnant to God.*

In psychotherapy, of whatever persuasion, self is strengthened to cope with those problems. Herein lies the basic problem with psychotherapy. With enough psychotherapy, some of the symptoms will respond so that the person may become better adjusted and the symptoms may either diminish or leave. But, in order to cope with those symptoms, the person builds better defense mechanisms and learns more acceptable behaviors, and self becomes stronger. Thus, when symptoms improve as a result of pure psychotherapy, the real problem, self-centeredness, *always* gets worse. This result is diametrically opposed to what God does, because God's way of dealing with *self* is that it must become weaker and weaker until its control is finally phased out. Self is reduced to nothing so that Christ can be everything. This is the process by which Christ becomes the center of the life, the basis of which is described in diagrams 7–9.

When Christ is in control (diagram 6), self, or flesh, no longer holds sway. It is not permanently replaced, but the Cross blocks the power of sin as we understand, under the tutelage of the Holy Spirit, the truth of Romans 6:11: "Likewise reckon ye also yourselves to be dead indeed unto sin, but alive unto God through Jesus Christ our Lord." We are still a unique self or individual, empowered by the life of Christ within. On the positive side, we *do* still have a personality. But when Christ is in the center of the life, he is in control. Paul wrote: "Let this mind be in you, which was also in Christ Jesus" (Phil. 2:5). He also wrote: "I can do all things through Christ which strengtheneth me" (Phil. 4:13), and "My God shall supply all your need according to his riches in glory by Christ Jesus" (Phil. 4:19). "All your need" includes emotional needs. And he will supply them not by a psychologist or a counselor but "by Christ Jesus."

When Christ is at the center of the life, he can meet all those needs as he has free rein to live out his life in us. Of course, Christ does not feel insecure or inadequate or guilty or have worries, doubts, or fears. So those things are progressively expelled from the life. If they are gone from the life, then we are no longer a bundle of frustration. If we are not frustrated, then we are not hostile. If Christ is at the center, when outer stresses occur, we do not react with hostility; rather, Christ in us responds just the opposite—with love, understanding, and compassion. And then, of course, if there is no frustration and hostility to be kept bottled up inside, there is nothing to adversely affect the mind or emotions. The mental and emotional symptoms are purged from the life. And if all that has caused the conflict inside is gone, the resulting psychosomatic symptoms leave also. This is usually experienced as a process, not as a crisis that occurs at a single point in time.

DIAGRAM 6

Naturally, if the body has suffered organic damage, such as a duo-denal ulcer, usually it takes time for that to heal. But many times we have seen instantaneous deliverance from such things as tension headaches, nervous stomach, and other pain caused by tension. When "the peace of God which passes all understanding" becomes the rule of life, then these things must go, whether the Holy Spirit does it gradually or more dramatically.

Now, the logical question is, How does Christ *become* the center of the life? What truth in God's Word explains this to us? In order to grasp this, it is necessary to think through another illustration, the *line diagram* (diagram 7). The horizontal line with an arrowhead at both ends represents eternal life, and, of course, eternal life has nei-ther beginning nor end. Only one Being has eternal life, and that is God. So, in reality, eternal life is Christ's life. At a point in time, and at an appointed time, he came to Earth and took on a human body as a baby, being virgin-born in Bethlehem. But the life that he lived in that body is the same life that he has always lived as God. He lived in a human body for about thirty-three years, and then he ended his earthly existence at the cross, where he bore our sins. He died, was buried, and rose again. And then his life continued.

At a later point in time, each of us entered into a physical existence by a physical birth. But when we are born, we are not in his life. Instead, we are in another existence represented by the line going through our parents or grandparents and their ancestors, all the way back to Adam. That is where our existence really began—in Adam. The hash marks in diagram 8 represent generations from our parents back to Adam. It is easy to see that we were in our parents before we were born, and they were in their parents. Therefore, if our grandfather had never had children, neither would we! Being in Adam, whatever happened to him happened to us.

We were *in Adam* positionally when he sinned. This is what made us sinners from birth. Paul explained, "Wherefore, as by one man sin entered into the world, and death by sin; and so death passed upon all men, for that all have sinned" (Rom. 5:12). Therefore, since we were *in Adam* when he sinned, we sinned. When he died, we died. So we are all born spiritually dead (Eph. 2:1).

When we were born, it was only natural to commit sin. We were born with a sin nature, or "old man," or Adamic nature. Paul emphasized, "All have sinned, and come short of the glory of God" (Rom. 3:23). We sinned, consistent with our nature, and our natural progress was downward. The diagram showing the life "in Adam" indicates this downward trend. This is verified by Paul's words: "The wages of sin is death [spiritually and eternally as well as physically]; but the gift of God is eternal life through Jesus Christ our Lord" (Rom. 6:23). Since we are born spiritually dead, our greatest need is life. We received physical life by physical birth, and we likewise receive spiritual life by spiritual birth (John 3:3; 1 John 5:11-12). The transition line depicts the truth propounded in 1 Corinthians 1:30: "Of him [God] are ye in Christ Jesus, who of God is made unto us wisdom, and righteousness, and sanctification, and redemption." The Spirit of God takes us out of the old Adam life and puts us into

Christ. Once we are *in* Christ, we are in an eternal existence, a life that is not based on time.

We have asked literally thousands of people this question: "What is eternal life?" Some reply, "It is life after death." Others may add, "I don't believe in it." When asked when it starts, they might reply, "When I die." Others may say that eternal life begins when they are saved, which is likewise incorrect. It didn't start when we were saved. Eternal life didn't start. It has always been! The truth is that once we have entered into the life of the Lord Jesus Christ, we have entered into *eternal life,* a life that spans the past as well as the future.

This new life traces back, not through our ancestors to Adam, but back through Christ to (and beyond) the Cross. Calvary is an event in eternity. Being *in Christ* means being in him eternally. Our life in Christ is an eternal relationship. Eternity is always present tense since it is not based on time. This means, then, we were in him *at the Cross.* We were in him not only when he was crucified but when he was buried and when he was raised from the dead and when he ascended into heaven. This identification is clearly established in Romans 6:4-6 and Colossians 3:1-3.

DIAGRAM 7

"Reconciled to God by the death of his Son" (Rom. 5:10a)

Hebrews 9:22b
Romans 5:8
1 Peter 2:24

John 1:14

John 1:1-2
Colossians 1:15-17
Hebrews 1:2-3

Hebrews 13:8

ETERNAL LIFE   (CHRIST'S LIFE)

"So by the obedience of one shall many be made righteous" (Rom. 5:19b)

The same truth is further stated by Paul's assertion, "I am crucified with Christ" (Gal. 2:20). We could not be crucified with Christ unless we were in Christ. Paul wrote that we were not only planted or buried with him but also *raised from the dead* with him (Rom. 6:5). Accepting Christ means that we are raised to a heavenly level of life. Scripture shows we are seated right now at the right hand of God *in* Christ (Eph. 2:6).

Paul turned our perspective back in time: "He hath chosen us in him before the foundation of the world" (Eph. 1:4). Like most spiritual truths, this may be difficult for our finite minds to grasp, but this eternal relationship is just as much true in the past as in the future, since time is not an issue.

This, then, is the manner in which Christ becomes the center of our lives. We are not only to understand this truth intellectually and theologically but also to enter into the experience of it by an act of faith. We are not referring to some experience where self or the flesh is permanently removed and we obtain sinless perfection; and we are not referring to what is sometimes termed a second work of grace. We are talking about entering into something experientially that is already ours positionally—the life of Christ. Though his life is a blessing received the day we are saved, we need to enter into the fullness of Christ, into the Spirit-filled life, into the abundant life, or into the abiding life, as the Bible variously terms it.

DIAGRAM 8

LIFE IN ADAM

Romans 5:12

PHYSICAL BIRTH

ETERNAL LIFE

"FOR AS BY ONE MAN'S DISOBEDIENCE MANY WERE MADE SINNERS" (Rom. 5:19a)

Romans 3:23

Romans 6:23 SEPARATION FROM GOD OR HELL

The difference it makes is that we cease trying to live for him and to work for him and to witness for him in the energy of the flesh. Once we discover by revelation or, better, by illumination, that we have been crucified and raised to new life, we can now reckon this to be so and let Christ live and labor through us. But this demands that we come to the end of ourselves and all our resources. "Not I, but Christ" is the way Paul expressed it (Gal. 2:20).

How can this awareness of "no longer I but Christ" take place? It happens differently in every life. But in point of time, it has to become as much a reality as the day we trusted Jesus Christ to save us. And it, likewise, is *by faith*. According to Scripture, we have to "reckon," or count, this to be so: "Likewise reckon ye also yourselves to be dead indeed unto sin, but alive unto God through Jesus Christ our Lord" (Rom. 6:11).

Reckoning, or counting, upon the fact of crucifixion and resurrection with Christ is an act of volitional choice or an invoking of the will to appropriate what God's Word states to be true of us in Christ. This is an act or decision of faith identical in all respects to that of trusting Christ as Savior. God's Word states that we are sinners and that the Lord Jesus Christ fully finished the work for our redemption at Calvary; we claimed this by faith, in repentance and surrender, and were born again. In the same way, God's Word (the same source) indicates that we are "selfers" (controlled by the flesh) and that we participated in his death, burial, resurrection, and ascension, and are thus free from slavery to sin's power.

Again, by volitional choice, we appropriate Christ as our Life just as we appropriated Christ as our Savior. In response to our act of faith in appropriating Christ as Savior, the Holy Spirit regenerated us in our spirit; in response to our appropriation of Christ as our Life, the Holy Spirit renews us in our minds (Rom. 12:2). The *will* is the vital function since the emotions may be at variance with the facts. As we choose against the world, the flesh, and the devil and count upon the indwelling Christ to be our life, we are choosing to have our minds renewed by the Holy Spirit. Consequently, our emotions are brought into congruence with truth (Eph. 5:18) so that we can "walk not after the flesh, but after the Spirit" (Rom. 8:4) and abide in him (John 15:5).

In some, this has occurred in a gradual way. As they began to understand their position in Christ and his life in them, there has been a dramatic transformation. Although this process was gradual, they *knew* that a new awareness of being in Christ had altered their attitudes in many ways.

DIAGRAM 9

Ephesians 2:6
Colossians 3:1–3

IN CHRIST (HEAVEN)

ADAM

SPIRITUAL BIRTH

Galatians 2:20
Romans 6:6

Saved by his life. Romans 5:10b
Risen with Christ. Colossians 3:1

1 Corinthians 1:30
John 1:12; 3:3
Romans 10:13

3000 years past

ETERNAL

LIFE

3000 years future

Ephesians 1:4

Romans 6:4–5

"There is therefore now no condemnation to them which are in Christ Jesus..."
Romans 8:1

HELL

We have also seen this identification-realization take the form of a dramatic and sometimes traumatic crisis as God began to make this a vital, living reality. The important thing is not how it takes place but that we are certain it happened—that it is now no longer "I" but Christ living and reigning within me. This process is described in greater detail in chapter 5.

To reiterate, we must realize that this identification awareness is an event that actually takes place at a point in time and experience. The process may be so gradual that we are not be able to identify that crisis point. But the result is unmistakable—self is dethroned, and Christ is enthroned. This, then, is the way we enter into the Spirit-filled or Spirit-controlled life; we enter in by way of the Cross through death and resurrection with Christ.

The reality of this does not have to take years and years after conversion. We may realize at the new birth that not only was he crucified *for* us but that we were crucified *with* him. As far as God is concerned, it is all true the day we trust Jesus Christ.

At our counseling office, we sometimes admonish people after they receive Jesus Christ as Lord and Savior: "Don't you ever *try* to live the Christian life! You have invited the Lord Jesus Christ into your life—let him live his life in you. That's why he entered your life." It is a life that is lived by faith. And, when we understand this, we see that there is no way we can live a Christian life. It is not a set of rules that we keep. That is legalism. It is the law that gives sin its power and spurs many believers on to overt or covert rebellion.

Valiant attempts to restrain sin from without rather than allow the Spirit to constrain from within often produce exactly the opposite results from those intended. Being enslaved by law is not freedom (Gal. 5:1). "Ye shall know the truth," Jesus promised, "and the truth shall make you free" (John 8:32). This kind of freedom is inviting Jesus into the life and then letting him live his life in ours. However, it is not a life of passivity but of aggressively yielding our will to his working.

If we are to struggle to live *for* him, then he cannot live *through* us. Until we deal with self, we continue the self struggle, perhaps even asking him to help us. We may spend effort and money for him. But this isn't the Christ-centered life. It is simply trying to harness the self life to work for God. During this time of trying—or this trying time—God uses us in spite of ourselves, but he cannot give us the Spirit-empowered ministry he wants us to have. He cannot multiply and master our ministry to the point where he is doing it through our yieldedness.

It is his goal, his purpose, that we should be conformed to his image (Rom. 8:29). If we are going to know this conformity, we have to be "made conformable to his death" (Phil. 3:10) and experience his

41

Cross. This is the only way that Christ can become our life initially, as well as perpetually. We must let him do the living so that he can work unhindered through our lives. The "Wheel of Life" chart explains how this can become a reality.

Are you ready to stop spinning your wheel so that Christ can become your center? Has God convicted you of the utter corruptness and sinfulness of the flesh? Unless and until we have seen this picture stand out in bold relief, we will not see the absolute necessity of denying ourselves and taking up the cross (Luke 9:23). If you are ready, just close your eyes, bow your head, and pray a *selfer's* prayer. Tell God that you surrender and that he can take over and do whatever he wants with you. Admit or confess that you have been attempting to live the Christian life in your own strength. Then claim by faith your death, burial, resurrection, and ascension with Christ. Thank God for saving you from yourself, and trust him to live his life through you. "Yield yourselves unto God, as those that are alive from the dead, and your members as instruments of righteousness unto God" (Rom. 6:13). If the surrender is unconditional, the responsibility for directing the life and the spiritual maturation process has been given to God. The time and matter of consummation will differ in each life. But God has promised, "Faithful is he that calleth you, who also will do it" (1 Thess. 5:24).

THREE

What Spiritual Maturity Really Means

The terms *spiritual growth* or *spiritual maturity* represent a very vague concept in the minds of most Christians. Many define a "mature" Christian on the basis of the things he or she does *not* do, much as a psychologist describes a "normal" person by the absence of symptoms. In other words, a person who is conscientious in observing certain taboos, such as drinking and smoking, and who actively participates in the ministry of the church is considered a "good" Christian.

Another common yardstick for measuring a person's spiritual growth is his prowess as a soul winner—introducing others to the Lord Jesus Christ. Of course, this does represent a degree of growth. And it is proof of new life, since we beget after our own kind. However, people can do witnessing, or soul winning, while self is still in control of life or, as the Scripture says, "after the flesh." This is supported by the fact that many Christians have never experienced the Cross and the reality of the Christ life as presented in the previous chapter. And yet, they are used by God in personal and corporate evangelism. While maturity is generally defined in terms of refraining from sinful activities and being involved in Christian service, frequently this has little or no spiritual significance in that there is relatively little permanent change in lifestyle.

Many Christians are in a sort of spiritual no-man's-land. They have no idea about how to proceed in spiritual growth even though they

DIAGRAM 10

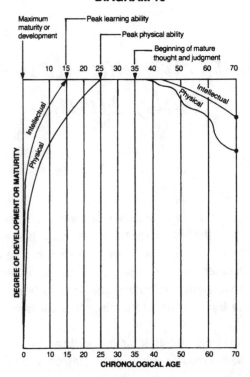

may have the motivation to do so. Since Spirituotherapy is basically counseling for spiritual growth, it is necessary to illustrate some guidelines that are valuable in objectively assessing progress in being "conformed to the image of Christ."

Diagrams 10 and 11 demonstrate some typical growth patterns in the lives of Christians and afford the possibility of comparison for the purpose of evaluating our spiritual lives. It should be understood that the growth patterns are representative of what is. They are not ideal in any sense of the term. It is certainly not God's will that we go for years or even a lifetime as a spiritual infant or adolescent. It is his desire that we go on to maturity. "Therefore let us leave the elementary teachings about Christ and go on to maturity" (Heb. 6:1, NIV).

For purposes of comparison, we have also added typical patterns for physical and intellectual maturity. The horizontal line at the base of diagram 10 represents our chronological age—our threescore and ten years that we may or may not be given. The vertical line at the left indicates relative growth or maturity. The upper horizontal line is indicative of the maximum maturity we attain in this life. Of course, this cannot be objectively measured, and it is different for every person. For the purpose of clarity in verbally explaining the chart, it is necessary to assign numbers to each of the spiritual (or carnal, as the case may be) patterns.

We will begin on diagram 10, with the path depicting the process of physical growth and decline. As represented by the zero, we are born and then grow rather rapidly for the first few months. The birth weight should be doubled in about three months and tripled in six. Then the rate of growth declines. If it did not, we would rapidly become giants. The peak of physical maturity occurs at about age twenty-five. After that, there is a gradual decline in physical vigor, along with the usual physical ailments, as the body begins to wear out. These are represented by the jogs in the right half of the line, with the life terminating at age seventy. In other words, after age twenty-five, things are bound to get worse unless they have been terribly bad before that.

Our intellectual growth is even more rapid, with the rate of learning peaking in the midteens. This remains fairly constant through our twenties and then begins to recede. As diagram indicates, we begin to attain more mature thought at about age thirty-five since we have made enough mistakes that we should have profited from experience. As we get older, we *should* get wiser.

If we could chart emotional maturity, we would find that emotional symptoms from our youth are amplified as the body begins to lose its reserve of physical stamina. In our younger years, we have sufficient strength to maintain our "fronts," or defense mechanisms, and to continue to be somewhat productive in our various life roles. As our physical strength wanes, we are faced with the fact that there is insufficient brain and brawn to fight the battles on the inside and the outside. Our responsibilities may deter us from "copping out" on external activities, but we are increasingly ineffective in maintaining our facade, and the emotional symptoms we have had all along become more glaring. This is the reason we see so many in their forties yielding to a variety of neuroses and "nervous breakdowns." The symptoms can no longer be kept under wraps.

DIAGRAM 11

Now, let us concentrate on the several lines represented in the spiritual state of man. At the bottom of diagram 11, the horizontal line depicts the "natural" man, or the man who has never been saved from his sinful state. There is, consequently, no change in his spiritual condition from birth. He is born estranged, or separated, from God and will remain so eternally unless he comes to know eternal life in Christ.

The vertical line at age ten represents spiritual birth or regeneration—conversion. We have selected this as the average age at which a person enters into a personal relationship with the Lord Jesus Christ.

At this point we must explain two other concepts—those of *position* and *condition*. These are often referred to as *standing* and *state*. It seems easier to distinguish between the two by using the former. As we look at the vertical dotted line from age ten, we see that it continues upward until it intersects the maximum maturity line at the top of the diagram. This is to indicate that in "0" time—immediately and eternally—we are considered perfect or justified in God's view. This is our *position* as Christians.

God sees us as dead to sin and the law (Rom. 8:2) and "alive unto God through Jesus Christ our Lord" (Rom. 6:11). Our position is perfect, since we have been given a standing in Jesus Christ (1 Cor. 1:30), and we are presently seated together "in heavenly places in Christ Jesus" (Eph. 2:6).

Although our spiritual *position* is perfect, our spiritual *condition* may be pathetic! The solid vertical line at age ten indicates some initial change in the life after conversion. But since most ten-year-olds are not gross sinners, there is usually not a great transformation in the life at the time of salvation. Looking to the right at line 1, we see that there is little positive change in the *condition* as time passes. This line represents the person who does not receive sufficient spiritual food (1 Pet. 2:2) and goes through life suffering from spiritual malnutrition. Even though he has been brought to life through a spiritual birth, there is little discernible growth toward being "conformed to the image of his Son" (Rom. 8:29). In fact, on the day he dies, he may be in a worse condition than the day he was saved because of the realization that he has wasted his entire life.

Line 2 illustrates the average garden-variety Christian. There is a period of little or no growth for a number of years. Then some growth begins during the teenage years. It continues as he (or she) takes on the responsibilities of parenthood, including taking the children to church. While the children are growing up, this person is active in church and performs some service. God uses him to some extent during this period of time, so he feels that he is a "good Christian." When the children leave home, he says to his wife, "Let's let the younger ones do it; we've done our part." He becomes inactive spiritually and begins to coast downhill.

After a number of months or years, he develops a twinge of conscience and decides to try again to be active. For a while the curve turns upward. There is an increase in activity and even some growth, but it is still not satisfying, so he goes down farther this time. Near the end there is a spurt of effort and spirituality as he crams for his finals. This path represents more defeat than victory, even though God honors the effort expended.

The other two lines, lines 3 and 4, represent Christians who have made a "total commitment" or have completely sold out to Jesus Christ. Line 3 describes the person who is concerned with service for Christ. He is a regular beehive of activity. He may be an active (or hyperactive) layman or minister who is involved in Christian activity morning, noon, and night. He is generous with his money as well as his time, proving that he has a real burden for the souls of others.

After a good number of years, usually, his defeats begin to outnumber his victories, and he falls back and regroups. He loses ground for a while and then changes churches or makes some other adjustment and charges ahead full force again. He gets a little higher this time, and while God may bless his service, this person has farther to fall and does so. He still has not recognized that most of his "accomplishments" are little more than sincere self-effort. So he gathers all his strength for one more gallant try. Failure this time results in the layman's dropping out of church or the pastor's leaving the ministry. God may bless and use someone who follows such a pattern, in spite of himself, but such a person never goes on to spiritual adulthood. It is always some sweet victory along with much defeat. It is an experience-centered life rather than a life of steady growth.

The final path, line 4, represents the believer who matures into spiritual adulthood. He, too, has yielded totally to the Lord Jesus Christ, but he is interested primarily in his growth rather than his service—in *being* rather than *doing*. As a result, he doesn't come on quite as strong as number three, but he is probably used of the Lord as much or more. He goes along at a steady rate of growth for a number of years, and he also begins to have problems. He feels that everything is going backward and that he is bringing reproach on the Lord's name. There may be physical problems, psychological symptoms, conflicts with children—these and many other things deplete a believer's self-resources and bring him to the end of himself. He is still going uphill but at a slower pace because he must come to utter helplessness. Only then is he ready for the Cross. The diagram positions this (the vertical line) at age forty because this is a conservative estimate of the average age at which a Christian enters into an abiding, abundant life of identification with Christ. This is not to say that a person cannot appropriate the Christ-life earlier. It is merely a statement of fact about present-day Christianity, at least in the United States.

Primarily because of ignorance, identification usually does not become a practical experience for many until years after the life has been totally surrendered to the Lord Jesus Christ. God uses adverse circumstances along with enlightenment in his Word to bring us to the end of our resources. We get so sick of ourselves that we cannot stand ourselves. Typically, only after we have reached this point does the truth of crucifixion with Christ and life in Christ produce a deep, dramatic transformation. Often the change in the life is much greater than at salvation. When we are saved, the sin is forgiven, but the flesh continues to pump out the sins. As with Paul in Romans 7, we are doing the things we do not want to do and not doing the things we do want to do. After identification, however, it is the Lord Jesus living his life through us—a totally different quality of life.

The transformation may be gradual or sudden, but it is real in either case. Occasionally there is a period of near euphoria because of the peace and freedom the person has realized. This may last for hours or days. But inevitably, self sneaks back into control, as represented by the dip after the peak has been reached. Since the person is down, with self back in control, he is a prime target for satanic attack. Satan always hits us while we are down! In fact, this is the only time he can really get to us. The first attack is usually hard on the heels of the identification realization. Being forewarned, we should be forearmed. The Word tells us that we should not be ignorant of

Satan's devices (2 Cor. 2:11), and also reminds us to "resist the devil, and he will flee from you" (James 4:7).

When we revert to self-control, the remedy is the same as when we realized victory in the first place—to reckon, count, or consider ourselves as dead to sin and alive to God (Rom. 6:11). It is not a onetime experience that insures constant victory; but rather, it must be a "daily" or "always" reckoning upon our deliverance to the cross. Jesus declared, "If any man will come after me, let him deny himself and take up his cross daily and follow me" (Luke 9:23). Paul expressed the same idea: "We which live are always delivered unto death for Jesus' sake, that the life also of Jesus might be made manifest in our mortal flesh" (2 Cor. 4:11). The cross spells death and deliverance as far as the reign of the flesh is concerned. We triumph always and only in Christ (2 Cor. 2:14).

After we experience a new sense of freedom as a result of entering into identification, we must have *assurance* of identification. This is parallel, to and just as vital as, being sure of salvation. Unless we have assurance of salvation, we will not possess our possessions in Christ. Unless we have assurance of identification, we cannot rest in the finished work of Christ. This is particularly important when we revert to self for the first time. Based on our feelings, we may be inclined to conclude, "I lost it. *I* won't ever have that joy again. *I* didn't read enough. *I* didn't pray enough." I, I, I—self in control and indulging in self-pity.

If we are certain that identification is a reality, we can be assured that we will never lose our stage of growth. We can no more go back across Jordan (as we will see in chapter 4) than we can go back across the Red Sea. After identification, however, the battles are more severe than before *if* we try to fight them in our own strength. If we do not have assurance based on God's Word and corroborated in our experience, we are very likely to think that our experience wasn't real and that we were kidding ourselves all the while. Just as we acknowledged our sins and were forgiven after salvation, we are now to acknowledge *self* and be "delivered unto death for Jesus' sake" that we might be restored in victory.

The only place of triumph is in Christ, not in self: "Now thanks be unto God, which always causeth us to triumph in Christ, and maketh manifest the savour of his knowledge by us in every place" (2 Cor. 2:14).

As long as the Lord Jesus is in control, we will be up. When *we* are in control, we will be down. In the beginning, there may be a transferring of control back and forth from self to Christ until we learn how to exercise our wills in faith, that he might more consistently live his life through us. This is a lifetime learning experience, but we gradually find it more supernaturally natural to permit him to retain control. The Word promises that "he which hath begun a good work in you will perform it until the day of Jesus Christ" (Phil. 1:6).

Appropriation of the truth of our identification with Christ does not constitute maturity. It signifies, rather, our becoming spiritually adult. It is very similar to age twenty-one, physically, at which time we become legally adult. But there is much maturing that must take place afterward. The ups and downs are some of the growing pains of maturing spiritually.

Referring to the curve showing the physical decline, we can now indicate some correlations. If we are maturing spiritually as we should, the physical decline is not fraught with nearly as many dangers from an emotional standpoint. As we lose physical strength, we can draw from the Lord according to our need. As we continue to draw from him, we can maintain our emotional stability while increasing in wisdom and favor with God and man. Conversely, when we are spiritual dwarfs and are continually harassed by the exigencies of life, our aging bodies are inadequate to cope with the emotional demands. This sets the stage for a neurotic break or a variety of escape mechanisms.

It should be pointed out again that there is no reason why it should be many years after salvation that we enter into spiritual adulthood. This is our birthright, and it can be possessed immediately upon experiencing salvation.

The ups and downs after identification are usually more violent in new Christians because of the lack of grounding in the basic principles of the Christian life. However, these new believers usually stabilize in a short period of time.

Which of the lines most nearly represents your life? Only as you are willing for the Holy Spirit to guide you in an objective assessment or spiritual inventory can you mature into a deeper and more wonderful relationship with our precious Lord. Don't stand still. Go on!

Abandon all rights to the helm of your life, and claim all that God is for all that you need, and he will make you what he intended you to be.

FOUR

When Life Is like a Wilderness

The previous chapter's depiction of a method of graphing spiritual growth has proven effective in helping troubled Christians assess their spiritual condition, or state. However, it was developed by man and must be accepted as such. This chapter has a similar purpose, but it uses a scriptural analogy, for which there is more than sufficient warrant.

The journey of the children of Israel from Egypt into Canaan affords a comparison for the stages of spiritual growth in the Christian. The Old Testament book of Joshua furnishes some of the most valuable illustrations of defeat and victory, and the New Testament book of Hebrews offers striking comparisons. Hebrews refers to Israel as an "example of unbelief" and carefully details the results of both belief and unbelief.

God deals with us as individuals in a manner similar to the way he dealt with the children of Israel as a nation. As shown in diagram 12, their progress went from Egypt, through the wilderness, to Canaan. God promised the land of Canaan to the children of Israel while they were yet in Egypt, just as he promises us a victorious life (Canaan) when we accept his Son, the Lord Jesus Christ. For four hundred years Egypt was a place of slavery for the children of Israel, and it represents the slavery of sin into which each of us was born. The Red Sea was the means of deliverance from Pharaoh's army for the children of Israel. When God opened the sea, the Israelites walked across on dry ground. In the analogy, the Red Sea is typical of our deliverance from sin and bondage through trusting the Lord Jesus Christ.

The wilderness was a place of wandering for forty years. All the Hebrew men over age twenty who came out of Egypt, except two, died in the wilderness because of unbelief and disobedience—including Moses, their leader. Joshua and Caleb were the two believing ones who took God at his word and went on into Canaan. Similarly, relatively few Christians enter the place of victory typified by Canaan.

The Red Sea is a picture of salvation; the Jordan River is a picture of identification with the Lord Jesus Christ. The children of Israel did not enter in because of unbelief (Heb. 3:19), and many Christians follow their example. They feel that God ran fresh out of miracles the day they were saved. It certainly took a miracle to open the Red Sea, and it takes a miracle of grace to change the human heart at salvation. It also took a miracle to open the Jordan River, and it is a miracle of illumination when we see that we are crucified with Christ and are set free from our "wilderness wanderings" to enjoy freedom and victory in the Lord. The victorious life is not a flowery bed of ease, but the battles are the Lord's *if* we let him fight them.

In my opinion, certain hymns and the theology they reflect have done a disservice to the spiritual growth of believers. Much of our theology can be shaped by the hymns we repeat so frequently. Thoughts such as "I won't have to cross Jordan alone," and "I'm bound for the Promised Land" leave the impression that the Jordan is physical death and the Promised Land is heaven. This being the case, many Christians long for the victory of heaven while never expecting any victory in this present life.

Now we have the setting before us. We can begin to evaluate our spiritual growth in light of this journey. It makes us much less apprehensive about the trip when we know the destination and are instructed concerning the pitfalls along the way. True, we must still cover the terrain, but we can chart a course that is attended by the least difficulty *if* we believe our map.

In a journey across dangerous territory a map is indispensable if we are to reach our destination. When I presented diagram 12 in a

DIAGRAM 12

EGYPT (THE WORLD)	RED SEA	THE WILDERNESS (WANDERING)	JORDAN RIVER	CANAAN (THE LAND)
1. Self in Egypt 2. Bondage to Satan 3. Sin 4. Conviction of Holy Spirit 5. Christ as Judge 6. Control by Satan	SALVATION	1. Egypt in self 2. Bondage to self 3. Carnality, immaturity, unbelief 4. Discipline of Holy Spirit 5. Christ as Savior and Lord 6. Coexistence with Satan	IDENTIFICATION	1. Self dispossessed 2. Bondage to Christ 3. Adulthood 4. Control by Holy Spirit 5. Christ as life 6. Overt assault by Satan
	His death for us as our *substitute*	That I may know him Phil. 1:29-30	Our death (crucifixion) in him as our *representative*	and the power of his resurrection
Grace through faith	Eph. 2:8-9 OBJECTIVE WORK	and the fellowship of his suffering Phil. 3:10 Grace through faith	Gal. 3:3 SUBJECTIVE WORK	(made conformable to his death)
PHYSICAL BIRTH				PHYSICAL DEATH

class, a man was overheard to say, "I wonder if I am closer to the Red Sea or to the Jordan." When this man saw a map of his spiritual journey, he was able to begin assessing his life. Not having realized that the Jordan was ahead, he probably thought that Canaan, or the victorious life, was heaven. As a result, he was unaware of the necessary preparation for crossing the Jordan; that is, experiencing the Cross.

Many Christians become very bitter when this preparation by adverse circumstances begins, because they are ignorant of the purpose of those circumstances. Their only recourse is to fight God rather than to cooperate with him and patiently endure "the fellowship of his suffering" (Phil. 3:10).

On a perilous journey we can be grateful for a map, but it is infinitely more comforting to have with us a guide who has made the trip before. Much of the apprehension is eased when the guide can prepare us in advance for the next segment of the journey and point out items of interest along the way. This is the purpose of the counselor in Spirituotherapy—to act as a spiritual director. In this manner, the counselor can point out the most direct routes and explain the stops and detours along the way.

Many times a person does not experience immediate relief from suffering, but he can accept it more patiently when he understands the reason for it. And if he knows that not only relief but deliverance lies immediately beyond that obstacle or trying circumstancee, it is almost joy to endure the pain. Now, let us begin tracing the spiritual journey from Egypt to Canaan. Beginning at the left of the diagram and proceeding to the right with each item, let us look at the progression as we consider various aspects of the Christian life.

First, when we are born, our entire being is in Egypt. This is the starting point for each of us. Then, when we are saved (or cross the Red Sea), we find that some of Egypt is still in us. The children of Israel looked back across the Red Sea and remembered the leeks and garlic they had there and gave Moses a bad time because they had only manna to eat. In the same way, we continue in some of the same thoughts and behavior that characterized us before we trusted Christ. This is due to the fact that self is very much in the ascendancy. Once we cross the Jordan (or experience the Cross), self is dispossessed. Although we must maintain the ground we have gained, by continuous reckoning, we never lose this stage of growth.

Second, the time in Egypt is a period of bondage to Satan, with him as our father and us as his slaves. After we have been Christians for some time, possibly many years, we begin to realize that we are in bondage to self. Paul described this vividly in Romans 7 in his admission that "the thing I don't want to do, I am doing; the things I want to do, I am not doing." His internal turmoil brought him to the frustration he vented: "O wretched man that I am! who shall deliver me from the body of this death?" (Rom. 7:24). He had seen self and its dominion in his life for the horrible thing that it is. It made him so sick he couldn't stand himself. That is great! Each of us must be brought to that same realization if we are to be willing to submit to the suffering of the Cross.

Until God turns on the searchlight of the Holy Spirit and illuminates his Word and our souls, we will not be "obedient unto death ... of the cross" (Phil. 2:8). Once God has dealt with in this manner, we are released from bondage to self to enjoy being bound to Christ, which is real freedom.

Third, our life during the time in Egypt is characterized by sin. We are born in sin, and we live in sin until the blood of Christ has dealt with the guilt of that sin.

Many Christians spend all their lives in the wilderness, and some who eventually go on into Canaan have spent the majority of their lives wandering in the wilderness. This is tragic but true.

The time in the wilderness is a time of carnality, of being controlled by self, or the flesh. The word *carnal* is often used in evangelical circles to describe a Christian who is living in open scandalous sin. This may be the case, but a devoted minister who is working his heart out for the Lord and has never experienced the Cross has self in the ascendancy and is still carnal, living and ministering in his own strength.

We might also label this as a period of immaturity—either spiritual infancy or spiritual adolescence. Assuming that we yielded to Christ as Savior and Lord at salvation and have continued to remain in a yielded condition, the length of time in the wilderness is determined by God. We should not apologize for being a spiritual adolescent any more than we should be ashamed of being a teenager. As long as we are yielded to him, he takes us through the stages of growth and maturity in a time and manner commensurate with his intended use of the completed vessel. We can delay the process by having an unyielded heart. If we stay yielded, it is the Holy Spirit's move. Many times during the process, it is necessary for us to be subjected to adverse circumstances so that our surrender is renewed, thus demonstrating God's sovereignty.

Finally, time spent in the wilderness can be a period of unbelief and disobedience, as it was with the children of Israel. They knew God had opened the Red Sea, but they didn't think he could open the Jordan. Many Christians forget that salvation is a miracle and do not expect God to continue his work of grace in their hearts. Therefore, they do not enter into the victorious or abundant life because of unbelief. Many do not even know that the Spirit-filled life is a live option for them. They seem to feel that it is reserved for only a select few who are God's pets and that they are destined to live a life of defeat, failure, and frustration. Poor teaching of progressive sanctification can nurture this stalemate in spiritual growth.

This is the result of both ignorance and unbelief—sometimes fostered by the erroneous teaching that the Jordan is physical death and that Canaan is heaven. As a result, people are conditioned not to expect victory and peace here on earth. They are taught that they must be saved, that they are going to heaven when they die, and that Christ may return at any moment. But in the meantime, it is just a mean time! The life of victory and power is for each of God's children. But resurrection power comes only after crucifixion, and few seem willing to submit to its suffering. Even though our death in Christ is an accomplished fact at our new birth, the experiential realization of it usually comes through anxious times. Suffering is a vital ingredient, as we see in Philippians 1:29: "For unto you it is given in the behalf of Christ, not only to believe on him, but also to suffer for his sake."

Fourth, the work of the Holy Spirit during the time in Egypt is to convict of sin. A thorough conviction of sin is essential before we will admit our need for the Savior. We must realize our sinfulness and lostness before we can be saved. After we trust the Lord Jesus, the work of the Holy Spirit is to discipline or teach us. Scripture uses the word *chosen* in this regard. The Scriptures say, "Now no chastening for the present seemeth to be joyous, but grievous: nevertheless afterward it yieldeth the peaceable fruit of righteousness unto them which are exercised thereby" (Heb. 12:11). When the discipline of the Holy Spirit has accomplished its purpose, we experience release from control by self and enjoy control by the Holy Spirit. This discipline could be looked upon as conviction of the flesh and as a parallel to the conviction of sin in the unbeliever. Such conviction is a necessary precursor to the Cross. We cannot be filled or controlled by the Holy Spirit until self and its hold are broken. And this is accomplished only by the Cross.

Fifth, during our stay in Egypt, Christ is our Judge. We are at enmity with God and remain so until we have been reconciled through the blood of the Lord Jesus Christ. Paul wrote: "God commendeth his love toward us, in that, while we were yet sinners, Christ died for us" (Rom. 5:8). Once we receive Christ (John 1:12), we become sons and are no longer at enmity with him. During the wilderness time, he is our Savior, and when we yield totally to him, he also becomes our Lord. This is one of the most important decisions a Christian ever makes.

This unreserved yielding to him is "our reasonable service" (Rom. 12:1) and is a prerequisite to our going beyond the Jordan and knowing the Lord Jesus as our very life. Paul said, "To me to live is Christ" (Phil. 1:21). This must take place by the illumination of the Holy Spirit. We can understand it intellectually, but the life of Christ becomes real within us as he is revealed by the Holy Spirit. Paul testified that "it pleased God, who . . . called me by his grace, to reveal his Son in me" (Gal. 1:15-16). The Lord Jesus Christ is revealed *to* us at salvation, but he must be revealed *in* us. Paul wrote that we "are always delivered unto death for Jesus' sake, that the life also of Jesus might be made manifest in our mortal flesh" (2 Cor. 4:11). Others cannot see him in our lives until first he has removed *us* out of the way.

Paul stated it another way: "My little children . . . I travail in birth again until Christ be formed in you" (Gal. 4:19). Christ cannot be formed in us until he has first dealt with the ugly self that resists conformity to Christ. Both the need and the answer must come by revelation (illumination) of the Holy Spirit. He must increase, and we must decrease. We decrease to nothing so that he can be everything—our very life.

Sixth, we must consider the work of Satan during the three periods of time. The time in Egypt is a time of total control by Satan. We are his subjects since he is the ruler of this world, and we are shackled by the bonds of sin, even though we do not recognize it until the Holy Spirit begins to draw us to Christ. During the wilderness period, we more or less coexist with Satan. He doesn't bother us very much because we are hardly worth his notice. Self is doing an excellent job of keeping things in a mess, so Satan just sits back and says, "Go to it, Self!"

The time in Canaan is an entirely different matter. We are promoted to the front lines, and those in the front lines of a battle are likely to become targets. Here we can expect direct satanic assault in a myriad of ways—attacks on our thought life, hindrances in our work, discouragement, sleepless anxiety, demonic harassment—varied, frequent, and subtle manifestations of the evil one. He is not stronger than our Lord, and he is a defeated foe, but we must not be "ignorant of his devices" (2 Cor. 2:11). To be ignorant is to invite trouble because he goes about "seeking whom he may devour" (1 Pet. 5:8).

It might do us well to take a look at the battles in Canaan so that we are not surprised or dismayed by the strife to be found there. Once the children of Israel were in the land, they still had to possess it, and they found it inhabited by seven tribes. The first battle to be fought in the land was the battle of Jericho. The siege of this walled city could have been a much greater battle than any they had fought in the wilderness if they had fought it with their own resources, depending on God for only a little help now and then along the way.

They did not approach it in that way—they followed God's directions explicitly, and as they made the final shout, the walls fell down without any effort on their part (Josh. 6:20). God had cautioned them not to take any of the "accursed thing" but to utterly destroy everything. But Achan, who was unwilling to be obedient, stole some valuables and hid them in his tent (Josh. 7:21). And the result? The next battle they fought was a different story—the army that went against Ai was defeated. They scurried back to camp to determine the cause of the defeat. God showed them Achan's disobedience and commanded that he and all his possessions be destroyed. In other words, self must be brought back to the cross in order that Christ might again be in control.

The next time the Israelites went into battle, God gave the victory as he promised (Josh. 8:1) because he was in control. God, not self, causes us to triumph (2 Cor. 2:14). Victory is always and only *his* work in and through us. Paul emphasizes that "we are more than conquerors through him that loved us" (Rom. 8:37).

At the lower portion of the wilderness section of the chart, there is the breakdown of the verse beginning with "that I may know him" (Phil. 3:10). Of course, we come to know him at salvation and continue to learn about him as we live with him. The next portion of the verse has been deliberately taken out of the order in which it appears in Scripture, so that it might fit in with the order of the experience of many believers. The "fellowship of his suffering" is our lot as we experience his Cross. Upon total commitment, the we begin the process that is so vital to our being forced to the Cross. After the work of the Cross in our lives, we can experience "the power of his resurrection." Only as we are at the Cross can his power be manifested—and we must daily be "made conformable to his death."

When he is in control, he can exercise his power and his glory. He will never share his glory with another (Isa. 48:11). All the power that God used in raising Christ from the dead is available in us (Eph. 1:19-20), which makes it imperative that "the excellency of the power be of him and not of us" (2 Cor. 4:7). God demonstrates his power as we yield to him so that we can't consume it or use it for the fulfillment of our own lusts. When we attempt to do this, he withdraws his power until we are again at the Cross and he can manifest himself for his own glory.

Now let's observe some other comparisons and contrasts. At salvation—illustrated by the Red Sea—we realize his crucifixion *for* us and appropriate his blood shed for our sins. At identification—typified by the Jordan—we realize our crucifixion *in* him and appropriate the victory his cross provides. Salvation is more of an *objective* work—something that is done for us. Identification is more *subjective* in nature—something that is done in us. In salvation Christ is our substitute; in identification he is our representative.

We entered into salvation by grace through faith; we enter into identification in precisely the same manner. Our salvation in all its states is grace at the beginning, grace at the end, and grace all the way through. We are not worthy to be saved from sin; neither are we worthy to be saved from self. But God in his infinite mercy deigns to have fellowship with us as redeemed sinners and to fill us with his life, love, and power in order that he may be glorified. Then, just as Joshua and Caleb spied out the land and came back with the minority report, we also must share with those yet in the wilderness the fact that the land of Canaan is indeed the Promised Land, flowing with milk and honey. However, like the faithful two, we must be prepared for rebuff, because few Christians are receptive to the command to "be filled with the Spirit" (Eph. 5:18), especially when they learn that they must first be emptied at the Cross.

It usually takes considerable time and study before we are sufficiently established in the new life to be able to share effectively with those who are yet in the wilderness. It seems that it takes most of a year for a person to be well enough grounded to be able to share with another without offending him. It usually takes considerably longer than that to learn to lead a person to the Jordan and go through the suffering with him as he proceeds downward to the Cross. The person himself must take this step of faith into the Jordan before the water parts, "for we which have believed do enter into rest" (Heb. 4:3). "There remaineth therefore a rest to the people of God. For he that is entered into his rest, he also hath ceased from his own works" (Heb. 4:9-10). "Come unto me, all ye that labor and are heavy laden, and I will give you rest" (Matt. 11:28). Those who are prepared by the Holy Spirit and have a clear view of the despicability of the flesh, or self life, and an equally clear view of its scriptural destiny, the Cross, are now ready to pray the "selfer's" prayer. An unsaved person controlled by sin is a sinner; a Christian controlled by self (the flesh) is a *selfer,* to coin a new term.

The unsaved person must concur with the scriptural conclusion that he is lost in sin and that Christ died for him and rose again. The carnal Christian must agree that there is nothing worthwhile in the flesh and that the scriptural remedy is that he died with Christ and rose again victorious over the world, the flesh, and the devil.

The sinner trusts Christ as *Savior.* The "selfer" trusts Christ as *Life.* We are reconciled to God by the death of his Son, but we are saved (from ourselves) by his life (Rom. 5:10).

FIVE

Intellectual Understanding— Then What?

You may be thinking, *This all makes sense intellectually and theologically, but how does it become a reality in* my *life?* But this is not just more knowledge to add to your collection of useless facts. This is the life that God wants for *all* his children, and he has no favorites!

So often we think that this all sounds appropriate for choice saints such as the apostle Paul, D. L. Moody, Hudson Taylor, and a few special others. But it is for *us!* While it is not *attainable,* it is *obtainable.* When we experience the Lord Jesus Christ as our life, we haven't really "arrived," unless it be at the foot of the cross. The cross was a place of humiliation, suffering, shame, and loneliness for our Lord. It will be the same for us—we are certainly not better than he!

You may also be prone to feel that this sounds plausible for others but that you are too far gone, or too worthless, for God to do such a miracle in your life. Well, here is good news for you. It is just such persons that God meets and sets free.

One lady came for counseling who had been diagnosed as paranoid schizophrenic and had spent time at a nationally known clinic and seven years in private psychiatric treatment. When the counselor told her point-blank that God would completely deliver her from all of these symptoms, she looked the counselor straight in the eye and explained her total disbelief that such a thing was possible. Fewer than four months and ten interviews later, God met her in a crisis experience and made a major change in her life.

Many tormented souls who come for counseling feel "It just can't possibly happen in *my* life." But God is faithful to his Word and his calling. He meets those who are willing to meet him. He has promised that he will draw near to us if we draw near to him (James 4:8). However, he doesn't promise to chase us down!

Some who come for counseling want their lives to continue pretty much as they are but without the problems they present. They may want *reformation* but are not willing to submit to total *transformation*. To be honest with them, the counselor must advise them that it may be necessary for them to endure more suffering. As long as they are trying to bargain with God, they might just as well forget it. When they are willing to drop their conditions and meet his, then they are candidates for victory and will probably continue in counseling until they are set free.

If we sincerely desire the peace and freedom that only God can give, we must be willing to commit ourselves first to the Lord and then to a concentrated study program. This is an integral part of the counseling process as well. Since it is our meeting with God, not with counselors, that is going to be our source of deliverance, we must spend time in his Word and in other books about spiritual growth.

After we have an intellectual understanding of our freedom, we must continue to study the Word to comprehend more clearly our position in Christ. As we do, and reckon, or count, it to be so, the Holy Spirit will make it real in our experience. As we stated earlier, it may be a gradual, dawning realization, or it may take some kind of crisis. Very possibly it will be even more real and transforming than the day we trusted Christ. Ours is to study and look to him. His is to reveal the life of the Lord Jesus in us.

As we begin to reckon upon these truths and God begins to deal with us, the ensuing struggle can take many forms. The remainder of this chapter describes some of the dilemmas that those in the counseling process regularly experience.

After Total Commitment

Some sincere and well-meaning Christian counselors or pastors lead people to believe that the lordship of Christ or total commitment is the epitome of the Christian experience. At times, this is true, because there are those who equate lordship with the walk in the Spirit. There is no problem with this, as long as the terms are clearly defined. The essential ingredient is the experience of the Cross. The question is, What is total commitment?

When a believer comes to our offices for counseling, we show him that any further progress in his spiritual maturity and subsequent deliverance from enslaving emotional symptoms is contingent upon his *total surrender*. The emphasis is on *total,* and we do not make it sound easy, because it is not easy! It means surrender with no reservations—not friends, family, profession, future, possessions, habits, sinful relationships, or lifestyle. Anything that we are or have or might be is included in such a complete surrender. If we are dead serious, we are going to be seriously dead! Our surrender is, basically, our permission for our Father to take us to the Cross.

Consider the story of the hen and the hog who were discussing the poverty program and what possible part they might have in the alleviation of hunger and suffering. Each made several suggestions, with the hen coming up with the idea that the world needed ham and eggs. The hog said, "For you that would mean a *contribution.* For me, that would mean *total commitment!"*

It is well to remember that such a commitment is an act of the will. The emotions may cry out against it, but the mind knows on the basis of God's Word that there is no other way. So, by a definite act of the will, we choose God's way for our lives, not having any advance knowledge about what this may entail. But knowing that his way, whatever it is, is the best way, we yield to him and trust him to bring it about in our lives (Ps. 37:5).

We must point out that this surrender and identification are not always simultaneous. In cases where a Christian is at his wit's end, learns of his position in Christ, and yields to God completely, the Holy Spirit reveals it to him, and it becomes real in his experience at once. This is the exception rather than the rule, however, in the average Christian's experience. The experienced counselor may see many clients surrender and appropriate Christ as life simultaneously, since he is dealing with a biased sample—those who are in dire need. Not everyone in the church is this dependent at the same point in time, or we would have a problem on our hands.

Generally, the condition of the counselee actually worsens after the inception of counseling and subsequent surrender. This is only logical, because God first has to take him through a process where he is reduced to nothing so that Christ might be everything—his all in all. But, again, if a person knows why he is getting worse, he does not push the panic button. He realizes the progress to the Cross is downward. Only when we understand the purpose of the suffering can we appreciate the "fellowship of his sufferings" (Phil. 3:10).

Many times total commitment takes place at salvation—which actually should always be the case—or shortly afterward. Then a person may go through many years of preparation for the Cross. If he is totally yielded, the length of time it takes for him to experience the Cross is determined by the sovereignty of God. And we can delay his work in our lives by hardening ourselves against his chastening (Heb. 12:11).

We have seen several people who were saved and who understood their identification with Christ at the same time. This resulted in in-depth work by the Holy Spirit, making the Christ life instead of the self life evident from the beginning. This is not to say that these people were immediately mature.

One such person was a young man who had recently spent four months in a mental institution. He was taking strong tranquilizers and yet was barely coping with life. He declared himself to be an agnostic but said he was willing to consider God's answer to his needs. In the first interview he yielded to the claims of Christ and was warned not to attempt to live the Christian life in his own strength. Returning the following day, he expressed ideas about how *he* should live the new life. This was exactly what we had instructed him not to do. He was again shown that it must be the life of Christ lived out in him.

That night he was planning to attend a ball game. Because of his paranoia, he usually needed a handful of tranquilizers to enable him to remain in a crowd. On this night, however, he had left his apartment and forgotten his tranquilizers. Because he hadn't been without them since he left the mental institution, he started back to get them and then thought, *The Lord doesn't need tranquilizers!* So he went on to the game, tranquilized only by God's Spirit, and enjoyed the best time he had experienced in twenty years.

Another young man was using LSD, speed, mescaline, cocaine, and marijuana from time to time, and his appearance matched his habit. He was born again in the first interview and set free from the drugs and his related lifestyle as the Lord Jesus became his life. He was discharged after the second interview. A short time later he began preparation for the ministry.

Assuming that we remain yielded to God's processing and shaping, the length of time depends on the way he plans to use our lives to his glory. We cannot effectively share with those who suffer if we ourselves have never suffered (2 Cor. 1:3-4). Our suffering is a time of learning and training for future usefulness. It can be an occasion for drawing closer to the Lord as he shapes his vessel, much as a potter molds his clay. As the Master Potter unerringly molds us more perfectly into the image of his Son, we are often prone to question whether these stages of shaping are really necessary.

Another significant point to keep in mind relative to surrender is that even though the surrender is total in scope, it must be carried out practically, item by item. In other words, we have surrendered the whole package, but God must now deal with everything in the package. Therefore, many times afterward, we find that we are still holding on to this or that. But he gently breaks our grip, unless we are stubborn. Then he must take stronger measures.

It is almost as if we are being literally carried to the cross, and we grasp for everything we pass on the way. But he that called is faithful (1 Thess. 5:24). In his sovereign love, he remembers our initial surrender and continues to bring his way to pass in our lives (Ps. 37:5). What comfort there is in this knowledge! Even though we resist him and think we have reneged on our commitment and missed his will for our lives, he is faithful to perform what he has begun in us (Phil.1:6).

Morbid Introspection

Almost without exception, many Christians, and those who fit the description of neurotic behavior, spend much time looking inward. They may be searching for sin or evaluating this or that behavior or trying to justify their existence. Those who feel exceedingly inferior and worthless may spend most of their time contemplating their hopeless plight. The result? The more they look inward, the more miserable they become, in spite of the fact that they may view their self-searching and self-condemnation as proof of their sincerity or as a kind of punishment by which they get even with themselves. They may conclude that God surely will reward them for their futile attempts to probe and purge and somehow make themselves acceptable in his sight.

This searching process is not only interminable and depressing to the believer, but it is also repugnant to God. The psalmist highlighted the fact that it is God's job to do the searching: "Search me, O God, and know my heart: try me, and know my thoughts: And see if there be any wicked way in me, and lead me in the way everlasting" (Ps. 139:23-24). The psalmist is praying, "*You* search me; *you* know me; *you* try me." But all too many Christians, by their actions, are trying to do the searching themselves.

At best, our searching can turn up only garbage, and sorting garbage is a most depressing avocation. In addition, if we could ever complete the interminable task, we would wind up with neatly sorted piles of garbage, but we would still be blind to the *source* of all the garbage—self. When God turns on the searchlight, he is much more interested in dealing with the source than with the results. And he is always ready to "forgive us our sins, and to cleanse us from all unrighteousness" (1 John 1:9). But it must grieve him to see us plagued by the same besetting sins year after year. He always abhors sin and desires to rid us of it by putting it under the *blood of Christ*. Self—the flesh—is also the object of his abhorrence, and he yearns to rid us of its control and dominion through the *cross of Christ*.

When an overly introspective person ceases or attempts to cease this useless and harmful indulgence of self, he usually feels guilty for falling down on God's job! And yet he always fails at it because he is playing God. That is a sure way to fail.

Spiritual Vertigo

This malady affects a great many Christians. The term is derived from a condition pilots sometimes encounter in which their senses tell them that their aircraft is in a totally different attitude from that indicated by their instruments. They may have been accustomed to flying by sight and by feel, so instrument flying presents a new challenge—they must fly by faith rather than by sight. They must have such complete confidence in their instruments that that confidence will override their feelings.

As Christians, we often face the same dilemma. If we are well adjusted psychologically, there is not as much disparity between our feelings and the facts. However, people who *feel* inferior, insecure, inadequate, and unacceptable are continuously faced with a set of emotions that are at variance with the facts or reality. Therefore, they must distort the facts to agree with their feelings (commonly known as a neurosis) or employ some defense mechanism to permit them to cope with an untenable situation. Someone has said that the neurotic builds castles in the air, the psychotic lives in them, and the psychiatrist collects the rent!

People may *feel* inferior when they really aren't. In fact, most who have extreme inferiority feelings excel in many areas. Because they *feel* inferior, there are many things they will not attempt, or they withdraw from certain situations—not because they cannot perform but because they *feel* they cannot. Naturally, this causes much frustration and internal conflict, and these are compounded because these people *know* with their mind that they can perform, but their emotions cry out No!

It goes without saying that we cannot change our emotions, but *in Christ* we are not called upon to change our emotions. This also is God's job, and if we try to do it, it is just so much more futile self-effort. When we experience the Lord Jesus Christ as our life, he changes our emotions as a result of renewing of our minds. All of these changes do not occur instantaneously. The transformation is effected by the Holy Spirit as we begin to place all of our confidence in "the instruments," the infallible Word of God. We must realize with our minds that God's promises are true and then determine with our wills to act upon them. God will honor his Word and keep his promises to us, even if we *feel* that they are untrue or that he won't keep them (2 Tim. 2:13). As we consistently *will* to place our confidence in our infallible "instruments," the Word of God, our feelings will increasingly come in line with the facts. When this happens, we no longer fit the label of neurotic, and our feelings are consistent with our faith in the facts.

Spiritual Surgery

Paul said that in Christ we are circumcised with the circumcision made without hands, in putting off the body of the sins of the flesh—the flesh, or self life (Col. 2:11). In his letter to the Romans, Paul wrote: "O wretched man that I am! who shall deliver me from the body of this death?" (Rom. 7:24). Then he proclaimed that the victory is "through Jesus Christ our Lord" (v. 25).

Here we find the identification truths, the experiential removal of self as the master of the life—much like physical surgery. The analogy has many similarities.

Before physical surgery, there is generally, though not always, a period of time during which a person suffers from certain symptoms. This suffering convinces him that there is a problem. These symptoms may plague the person in various forms for several years before a physician is seen or surgery actually takes place. Often the patient will try several remedies that suppress the symptoms, in a vain effort to avoid surgery. When the adverse effects on life are severe enough and the pain is no longer tolerable, the person realizes that something more must be done.

Christians try everything from hedonistic pursuits to compulsive Christian service. Or they may hit the tranquilizer bottle or seek spiritual "experiences" of various kinds. They try anything in order to avoid the spiritual surgery that must take place if they are to be set free and unhindered in their service for the Lord. This is similar to patients who try every other remedy and escape until surgery becomes unavoidable. Even after they know that surgery is the only way out, most people postpone it as long as possible.

Once they have a diagnosis, patients experience some relief if they know that the problem is not terminal. There will be pain involved, but their lives will be normal again after convalescence. Understanding the suffering removes the mystery even though the pain persists. The problem can now be dealt with realistically. We understand that whatever adverse circumstances we are experiencing, it is permitted by God to point out the necessity of spiritual surgery. God does not allow this to punish us but to discipline or chasten us so that our lives may be more free and joyful than before (Heb. 12:11).

Once all the escapes are blocked off, we must endure the surgery. As the surgeon makes preparations for the operation, the patient must be rendered helpless. You can imagine how ludicrous it would be for the patient to jump around on the table in an attempt to "help" the surgeon. If the patient begins to stir during the surgery, more anesthesia is administered. The surgeon neither wants nor needs the patient's help.

In a similar manner, as God prepares us for spiritual surgery, he must take us through the process of defeat, failure, and suffering to render us helpless so that he can do his work. Usually, we have done so much to "help" him that we want to continue doing so as he begins the process (Rom. 6:11). The surgeon of the body uses the scalpel. The Surgeon of the soul applies the Cross to the source of the problem—*self*.

The divine Surgeon's purpose is not merely to take away the pain and restore us to our former way of life, in which self dominated, but to enable us to enjoy the reign of the Christ life instead of the self life. Sometimes the surgery is short, and sometimes it is lengthy, depending on the case. In other words, the spiritual surgery may take place gradually, or it may be a crisis experience. In either event the result is the same—a transformation of the life by the renewing of the mind (Rom. 12:2).

After the surgery comes convalescence. This is rarely a smooth, uphill process. There are many ups and downs as we adjust to the new life. We may often revert to the old life with its defeats and frustrations—only to require a repeat of the surgery of the Cross (Luke 9:23; 2 Cor. 4:11).

Finally, as in physical surgery, we delight to tell others of our successful surgery, and we are more than delighted to recommend the eminent and only Surgeon so that our friends may also know the joy and the rest found in the new life—the Christ life.

Putting Suffering in Perspective

Meaningless suffering is agony in the extreme. The physical pain may not in itself be unbearable, but the mental anguish becomes a cruel taskmaster. When misunderstood, suffering causes despair, defeat, and frustration. Often it is accompanied by resentment, bitterness, hostility, and depression. However, if we can apply God's lenses to our eyes and see the goal he has in view, then we are afforded an entirely new perspective on the suffering. We may have endured untold suffering for years. But when we come to appreciate it as the "fellowship of his sufferings," we recognize in retrospect that suffering is indeed a privilege (Phil. 1:29).

One lady who came for counseling had, like the woman in Mark 5:26, "suffered many things of many physicians." She recited her story about spending fifteen years with psychologists and psychiatrists, Christian and secular, in addition to making the rounds of ministers and counselors. By the time she came to us, she was almost nonfunctional. The counselor's comment on her condition was simply "Wonderful!" The woman gave the counselor a look of amazement, not amusement. But as she was shown the necessity of coming to the end of self, she began to see that empathy, not sympathy, was what she really needed. Years of other treatment had merely served the purpose of driving her farther down.

God used these circumstances to force her to the end of self. Realizing the reason for her suffering, she quit fighting God and trusted him to continue it until he had accomplished his purpose. She cooperated with him as he rapidly took her to the Cross. In a very short time, she was released from the so-called mental illness for which she had endured years of symptomatic treatment.

The Death Blow

Suffering takes place over a period of time as the Cross does its work. Yet there must come a time when self yields completely to the Cross. There are many signs of the end's approach. Usually there is a period of deep anxiety just prior to the end. As in physical death, sometimes there is sudden "death" without a struggle. In other cases, there are the death throes as life leaves the body. Even though a patient may be dying of cancer and actually yearns to die because of the excruciating pain, as he begins to die, he instinctively tries to hold on to life. Similarly, even though a believer realizes that he is being drawn to the Cross, it is almost as if the Lord has to drag him all the way, while the person clutches at everything he passes.

If we have presented our bodies to the Lord as "a living sacrifice" (Rom. 12:1), he is not going to heed our pleas for comfort until the sacrifice is consummated. The Father had to refuse to ease the awful agony of his Son on the cross as he cried out, "My God, my God, why hast thou forsaken me?" Just so, he cannot—he *must not*—ease the burden until his gracious work is finished in our experience. The Lord Jesus had no respite from his sufferings until he died. And it was only after the suffering that Jesus entered the resurrection life.

Those who would relieve our symptomatic pain through ill-advised counseling can do us a disservice. It would be similar to offering relief to someone who is actually being crucified. If he were taken down, patched up, given food, water, and blood transfusions and then put back on the cross, he could be kept alive for an extended period of time. But if he has to die, prolonging his suffering is not doing him a favor.

In our spiritual journey, the suffering of the crucifixion precedes the power of the resurrection. Paul gave the assurance that "if we suffer, we shall also reign with him" (2 Tim. 2:12). We cannot bypass the Cross and still know its power, nor can we experience the Cross without its suffering. The theology of the Cross cannot substitute for the experience of the Cross in our lives. It is much more romantic to read about the trials and tribulations of great saints as God prepared them for ministry than it is to experience this preparation ourselves.

Even though the atonement for sin was vicarious in that Christ shed his blood for our sins and, in so doing, gave us his life, his cross must become the *experienced Cross* before his victory and power can be ours. In other words, we must enter into his life before we can share his death. Or to say it another way, it is through entrance into his life that we become partakers of his death. As the corn of wheat must fall into the ground and die to produce fruit, so also must we enter into his death before his life can be manifest in us in the bearing of much fruit (John 12:24; 15:5). "Whosoever will save his life shall lose it" (Luke 9:24).

As we approach the Cross, we must be brought to the utter end of our own resources. As this happens, there are times when we think we cannot go on—that God doesn't love us or he wouldn't let us go through these difficult times. Or we may suspect that our unsaved or saved mate is bringing all of this on us or that it is the result of our sin (and it may be). We may even conclude that God delights in punishing us—perhaps because we do not have enough faith. All of these thoughts and many others may surge through our minds as we near the end of self.

Many times we try to "rescue" ourselves from this because we dread the pain or humiliation. One by one God eliminates the avenues that offer some temporary relief. When we fear that there is no way out but death, we have arrived at the truth. There isn't!

However, suicide isn't the answer because the problem is not confined to the body. It has invaded the soul. Suicidal feelings are not at all uncommon during this period of time since we feel that our faith is so weak that even God could not possibly do anything in our lives. But in his grace, he made a way by which we can get rid of ourselves and yet stay here. That way is the Cross.

We have been brainwashed to think that we must have greater and greater faith if God is to accomplish anything in and through our lives. In practice, however, we find that our faith becomes progressively weaker and weaker. Occasionally the physical strength is also diminished to the point where a person is all but immobilized. This is necessary so that God can get us out of his way until he can complete the work. One woman expressed it this way: "I'm so weak I can't even *help* God!"

Another woman in this situation discovered one morning that she could not get out of bed. Her husband notified our office that he would have to call a psychiatrist. After additional conversation, he agreed to bring her to the office. She limped into the counseling room and slumped into a chair. Only with great effort could she converse. When asked if she knew what was happening, she replied, "I think he is finishing the work." The counselor agreed. Then she said very slowly, "I'm just afraid I will get in his way as I have in the past, and he will not complete the work."

"You don't have to worry about that," she was assured. "He isn't even going to give you enough strength to get in his way!" She thought about that for a moment and then replied with measured words, "That's the happiest sad thought I ever had!" The counselor then shared this verse with her: "Even when we are too weak to have any faith left, he remains faithful to us and will help us, for he cannot disown us who are part of himself, and he will always carry out his promises to us" (2 Tim. 2:13, TLB). She received no strength until a day or so later when God set her free. His strength was made perfect in her weakness (2 Cor. 12:9).

The New Life

When the process of this crucifixion experience is consummated, the result is spiritual resurrection life. Though it may be a gradual or a crisis revelation, the transformed life with its freedom is the proof that the Christ life has become a reality. The manifestation of his life is different in each person. It usually takes several months for a person to become reacquainted with himself and to have some idea of what to expect by way of reaction to various circumstances. Many have made the statement, "I just do not know myself anymore." The reaction of family members is much the same. Some spouses experience a state of mild shock as a result of being conditioned by past experience to expect unchanged behavior.

Although this stage of growth is never lost, the victory or joy of it may be, as self returns to the ascendancy in the life. It is most difficult not to return to past patterns of behavior and "try to live the Christian life." It is well to memorize and claim Galatians 2:20. Then, at the beginning of each day we can reckon ourselves, again and consistently, to be dead to sin, and trust the Lord Jesus Christ to express his life in us. The will must be engaged at all times. We *will,* and he empowers (Phil. 1:6).

Throughout the day we do well to remind ourselves several times, "It is not I, but Christ" and to expect that he will govern our plans and actions. We are not to become introspective and test every thought and action to see if Christ or self or Satan is responsible for them. We are merely to commit the day and our life to God and trust him to control us and each situation to his glory. *Committing, trusting, reckoning*—all of these terms are indicative of a functional will.

It is important to realize that if we regress to the point where self is in control, the defeats we suffer may be valuable learning experiences—if we are determined to see them as such and not panic at our loss of victory and the hurt to self.

Many experience more "down" time than "up" during the early weeks of the deepened relationship, as they gain discernment concerning the reassertion of self and the attacks of the adversary, which are certain to come.

The excitement of life under Christ's control makes each day a new adventure when we are at rest and trust him, who is our life, to cause "all things to work together for good" (Rom. 8:28).

Checkup Time

A diagram similar to the one in chapter 3 has been meaningful in my attempts to explain some of the concepts we have discussed in this chapter. It is similar, but it is a bit less cluttered and easier to apply to life. While it is important to understand the psychological and inter-personal conflict that might be troubling us, it is much more impor-tant to get behind those things and deal with the real issue—the identity out of which we are living, which tends to perpetuate the self-defeating thoughts, feelings, and behaviors.

Diagram 13, on page 81, might be used to help someone chart his own testimony, to make a spiritual map that depicts the road over which he has traveled, and perhaps to gain a preview of what may lie ahead. But even a perfect map will do us little good if we do not know where we are.

Some years ago my wife and I were in Kansas City with some of our relatives. It was dark, and we became lost. We pulled over to the curb, under a streetlight and spread the map out on the hood of the car to study it. We had a good map of the city and a car in excellent running condition, with plenty of fuel. But the map was useless un-less we could find our location on it. What we needed was someone to put an X on the map and say, "You are here."

The same is true of our spiritual road map. We must know where we are if we are to know where we are going. We may be looking ahead for something that is already behind us. One woman, for ex-ample, had been immobilized with depression, despite many ses-sions with psychiatrists. Some years later, and before I met her, she attended a conference at which God transformed her life. For sev-eral weeks she experienced victory that neither she nor her hus-band could believe. However, without a spiritual foundation, she soon lost the victory and reverted to her old behavior patterns. Since she wasn't sure what she had lost, she didn't know how to regain it.

Later she shared her story with me, and I was convinced that she had experienced the exchanged life but had no instruction as to how to continue her walk in the Spirit. Putting it in terms of chapter 1, she had relinquished her "baby" but had never owned him. During the course of counseling, she was able to appropriate with knowledge what God had done for her, and she learned how to continue in vic-tory.

Another way to consider this diagram is to think of how we would give our testimony about the significant mileposts along our spiritual journey. Most of us will have little trouble understanding the first milepost, marked "Salvation," since many messages are preached on that vital subject. And it isn't too difficult to understand what it means to make a "total surrender" of the life, the second milepost (though it is often difficult to do).

However, the third milepost, "Identification," or "the Exchanged Life," may not be as easy to understand. Suppose, for instance, that your pastor asked you to give your testimony at a Bible study he was leading. You might reply, "Sure, I am always ready to testify for my Lord." But the pastor goes on to add a stipulation regarding the content of the testimony. He asks you to omit all reference to the time when you were born again, because those in the class are already believers. He then says, "I would like for you to share with the class how God brought you to the utter end of yourself and what kind of mess you were when you got there. Then tell them how the cross of Christ became a reality, whether gradually or suddenly, and what the resulting transformation was like. Further, if I asked your parents, spouse, children, and friends to corroborate that testimony, could they?" In other words, the pastor was asking for a "before and after" testimony. What would be your response?

While such a testimony is not absolutely necessary for the cross of Christ to have become a reality in our lives, it is helpful in sharing with others if we are able to retrace our own steps to and through the Cross. The diagram will not fit anyone precisely, but it may give us some idea of how we might portray what God has done in our lives, at least at the three basic junctures of "Salvation," "Total Surrender," and "Identification."

The first *X* on the road map is at "Salvation," which follows a period of conviction of sin, when the Holy Spirit is drawing you to Christ. At this point you should ask yourself, *Have I truly been born of the Spirit?* If that has not occurred, you should settle this matter with the Lord before going on.

If you are able to put an *X* there, what has been your life experience since that time? Were there changes that reflected your new life, and how long did they last? Did you understand, at the time, the ramifications of a total surrender to Christ as Lord, or was there another time when you took your hands off your life totally?

I asked this question of an engineer who had been a believer for a number of years. He replied, "I will have to walk around the block a few times before I can answer that." He "walked around the block" for approximately six months before he returned. But when he did return, he was ready to do business with the Lord.

If you have reached the point of "Total Surrender" to the Lord, you can put an X there. At this point on the diagram, three paths are open. It would be preferable to take the center path, to appropriate by faith the blessings that come from "Identification" with Christ. Many believers in the counseling setting enter into victory simultaneously with surrender, since the counselor teaches them about the experienced cross. This is because many who come for counseling are in desperate straits, which makes them prime candidates for the crisis intervention of the Holy Spirit. Therefore, average Christians might take longer to appropriate victory since many of them aren't forced to look for immediate answers to critical problems.

81

Our total surrender is somewhat like the Lord's experience in the Garden of Gethsemane, where he said, "Not my will but thine be done." His surrender was valid, but it was several hours before he actually endured the cross. Our "Total Surrender" could be termed our personal Gethsemane—in which we grant the Holy Spirit our permission to make the Cross a reality in our experience.

It may be, however, that your surrender to the Lord was not accompanied by an entry into victory but rather resulted in an attempt to try harder to make the flesh serve God. This would be represented on the diagram as the uppermost pattern, which leads to frustration and defeat. Self-effort doesn't work much better after surrender than before. Coming to the end of self is never easy and is frequently painful. But it is extremely profitable if you learn the lesson that the Holy Spirit has patiently tried to teach you. If you can give testimony of having gone to the Cross in your experience in a manner similar to this, place an *X* at the cross on the upper pattern.

Or maybe you surrendered at some time in the past only to find that things got worse. You may be following the lower pattern and are about to go even lower. This is perhaps the more common pattern in the lives of believers, since most seem to grope their way through life by trial and error. When the pain increases, as depicted by the ups and downs, the flesh tries to calm the rough waters. The arrows pointing back to the place from which we came indicate our effort to try to do more of whatever brought us relief, however fleeting, in the past. Just as with using drugs and alcohol, it takes more and more of the activity to tone down the insatiable demands of the flesh.

Of course, all the things we do to alleviate the pain are couched in terms of self-effort, which is our basic problem in the first place. Such efforts are doomed to fail, but since we don't yet realize that reckoning ourselves dead to sin is the only way out, we do all *we* can do to avoid the Cross. One of the first and most common things we do is to try to find victory through zealous applications of the disciplines of the Christian life. Now there is, of course, nothing wrong with Bible study, Scripture memory, prayer, regular church attendance, and church work. But such efforts accomplish little for us if we are trying to find victory through *trying* instead of *dying*. Therefore, as needful as these disciplines are, God won't honor our attempts to strengthen the flesh.

Many have discovered how futile it is to seek victory through their own efforts, even in the church, and have turned to other avenues to find meaning or relief from their inner turmoil. Many seek relief in self-help programs that can be found in the world or in some Christianized editions at the nearest Christian bookstore. There is no doubt that some of these work, at least for a while. They are exactly what they claim to be—self-help, an attempt to increase the confidence in the flesh.

When the self-help programs don't work, some believers turn to covert sin—to drinking, immorality, or other sinful pleasures. Of course, these only make the problem worse, as the believers add guilt to whatever turmoil they experienced in the first place.

When a person has exhausted all that he knows the church teaches, the self-improvement programs, and possibly some rebellion, he may turn to some kind of counseling or therapy. Of course, he would want to choose a Christian therapist so that he might not be given advice counter to his beliefs. As we can see in the diagram, God has us programmed to go to the bottom—to the end of our resources—that we might deny ourselves and take up the cross. If the Christian is in therapy, rather than Christ-centered and cross-centered counseling, the therapist will unwittingly be saying, in effect, "Not if I can help it, you won't." And by impeding the believer's downward progress through alleviating the symptoms only, the therapist has done the suffering believer a disservice. He is now stronger and can handle things better by himself. Yes, the *symptoms* may be better, but the *problem* is worse. It may take more adversity next time to bring him to the end of his fleshly resources. This doesn't mean that his therapist was intentionally sabotaging the believer's progress. However, if the therapist has not been to the Cross in this sense, it is obvious that he would not practice an approach that leads others to the Cross. The downward progress can be summarized under the rubric of "conviction of the flesh." Only as we see the flesh for what it is will we see the absolute necessity for the Cross to become a reality.

What about it? Can you put an *X* at the cross, or are you still on your downward trek? It can be a relief to know why you are where you are. At least you know where to go from there and that you can't do it by self-effort. Understand that the giving up and letting go can take some courage, since you are denying yourself the right to fix yourself.

As you place the *X* on your spiritual road map, remember that waiting passively for the next signpost to appear will all but guarantee a major delay in your spiritual growth. Just as in driving a car, the signposts come up as you move along—not while you are standing still. Faith is the dynamic that fuels the movement. It is by grace through faith that we are saved from sin, and it is also by grace through faith that we are saved from ourselves.

As we get to the point of appropriation, emotions may play a major part in resisting our ability to lay hold of our victory in Christ by faith. Many have not discerned the difference between the activity of their minds and the activity of their emotions. If there is emotional damage, the emotions may be totally unreliable. In this case, it is necessary to take action by faith, an act of the will, on what is *known* to be truth from the Word of God.

It is possible, then, to bypass damaged emotions and experience a renewing of the mind, which will in time result in the healing of emotions. What you *know* will eventually change the way you *feel.*

Suppose that you are driving down the interstate in your new sports car and you decide to see how it feels to drive considerably above the speed limit. You set the cruise control to 120 miles per hour and sail along, listening to your stereo, and everything seems wonderful. However, in the rearview mirror you see a car with a blinking red light. What you know (mental) causes some peculiar feelings (emotional), and in a split second, there is a sensation in the stomach (physical). Without too much prompting from the car behind, you begin to slow down to 100 and 80 and 60 and are preparing to pull off the road. But just at that moment, the policeman receives a radio call advising him of an accident up ahead, so he accelerates and leaves you in order to go to the accident. Now, does your internal situation reverse itself just as quickly as the onset of the symptoms occurred? Or does it take a while for all the feelings to subside? More than likely, you can answer from the crucible of your own experience. What you knew about the police car affected the way you felt almost instantaneously. But when you realized that you escaped getting a ticket, the symptoms gradually dissipated. What you know will change the way you feel, but not always immediately. It is just so in our emotional makeup. Feelings that have been in place for a lifetime will respond to the renewing of the mind, but we must allow time for the process to take effect.

As you consider where you are in your spiritual journey, has the Holy Spirit shown you what you are holding on to that is impeding your downward progress? It could be that there is some pet sin, a relationship, a possession, an inadequate concept of God, or an old fear (maybe the fear of freedom or of failure or of losing control)—any or all of these can thwart our progress and cause us to be defeated.

If God is in control, we must lose control. And as long as we are in control, we are really out of control. The willingness to lose control of all our circumstances is prerequisite to our finding our identity in the Lord Jesus Christ. Someone has aptly observed, "We never know that he is all we need until he is all we have." The fear of losing control, even though what we are doing is not working, is probably the greatest fear that any of us faces. The prospect of losing the familiar, even though painful, for that which is unknown can be a frightening prospect.

Loss of identity can be totally demoralizing and depressing and can even result in psychotic episodes. Some years ago I was called to a distant state to counsel a young man who had become psychotic. He had been hospitalized because he was out of touch with reality and was on massive doses of tranquilizers. He had planned to be a physician, but he had failed his examination to enter medical school. His entire identity was wrapped up in what he was to become, and when that was denied him, he could not handle it and broke with reality. Underlying identity problems brought on his mental symptoms.

In a similar situation, I saw a young man who had been a high school basketball star and won a full scholarship to a major university. All was well until he damaged his knee in the closing game of his high school career. He ended up in a hospital psychiatric ward. Even though he was handsome, he was convinced that his face was grotesque. Since he had lost everything that meant anything to him—his identity based on basketball—he was unable to tolerate it and broke with reality.

A businessman had spent most of his waking hours building several businesses. A series of events caused him to go bankrupt, and the consequent loss of identity caused him to wind up in a mental institution.

Losing identity when a person has nothing with which to replace it can cause massive damage to the self-concept, and few can tolerate it. However, God does not ask us just to lose our identity but to exchange it for one that will work both for time and eternity. Whatever we have previously seen as our life must be given up if we are to know Christ as our life. We must lose our life in order to save it. Jesus said:

> Except a corn of wheat fall into the ground and die, it abideth alone: but if it die, it bringeth forth much fruit. He that loveth his life shall lose it; and he that hateth his life in this world shall keep it unto life eternal. (John 12:24-25)

A parallel passage reads: "Whosoever will save his life shall lose it: and whosoever will lose his life for my sake shall find it" (Matt. 16:25). I do not believe it is doing violence to Scripture to substitute the word *identity* for *life* and make the passage read: "Whosoever will save his identity shall lose it; and whosoever will lose his identity for my sake will find it."

Laying down our lives is not really an option—it is a command. "Reckon ye also yourselves to be dead indeed unto sin, but alive unto God through Jesus Christ our Lord" (Rom. 6:11).

Missionary martyr Jim Elliot caught the meaning of this when he wrote in his diary: "He is no fool who gives what he cannot keep to gain what he cannot lose."

We should not construe the loss of self and identity and control as a onetime appropriation that results in uninterrupted victory. The ups and downs in each of the three paths after the cross on the diagram are indicative of the fact that the believer must take up the cross daily and continually. In the following chapter, we'll look at the anatomy of these "downers" along the path and the way back to victory.

SIX

The Great Exchange

In chapter 2 we looked at two lives, the Adam life and the Christ-life, and in chapter 5 we addressed the process of experiential appropriation of Christ as our life after intellectually understanding the reign of the flesh and the answer, the experienced Cross. In this chapter, we will look at two identities—one assigned by the world and one delineated in the Scriptures.

The identity assigned by the world is imbibed as we develop as persons and begin to view ourselves as others see us or as we *think* they see us and, sometimes, as we would *like* for them to see us. This assessment of ourselves may be totally unrealistic, positively or negatively; we may think too much of ourselves or too little. In either case, it is an identity built on *people* (positive or negative), *performance* (good or bad), *possessions* (little or much), *power* (or lack thereof), and our *past* (good or bad). Such an identity is based on *doing* for ourselves, others, and God in our own strength. In other words, we are *doing* (or *not* doing) in order to *be*.

The identity delineated in the Scriptures has nothing to do with the way we see ourselves in relation to others or what our behavior is or has been; it is an identity based on being *in Christ* and finding our life in him. Any performance involved is *his* performance at Calvary; on our part, it is *being* instead of *doing*. In other words, as we identify ourselves with the Lord Jesus Christ, we begin to live out of our new and true identity in him.

Such an identity is not *earned*—it is *learned* as it is taught by the

Holy Spirit; it is not *attained* by works—it is *obtained* by faith. Although theological understanding is usually involved, there is no practical change in the life until illumination of the truth of being in Christ is applied by the Holy Spirit. Teaching, preaching, and discipleship can be very helpful; but in the final analysis, one's identity is first and foremost a work of the Holy Spirit.

While the identity assigned by the world is based on *doing,* the identity delineated in the Scriptures is based on *dying* and being resurrected with the Lord Jesus. As we have seen in the foregoing chapters, we must lose our life or identity, assigned or developed in the world, at the Cross if we are to find our life or identity based on our being in Christ in heavenly places and living the resurrection life (Matt. 16:24). However, believers are not naturally prone to stand in line at the cross to die. It is much more palatable to gain an intellectual understanding of our identity in Christ and to attempt to live out of it without going through the agony of the cross. This, of course, is doomed to fail since the flesh is incapable of living Christ's life. Christ's life is resurrection life, and it proceeds from the crucifixion—first for our Lord and then for us.

We might illustrate the worldly, or fleshly, identity we have just described with the following diagram:

DIAGRAM 14

LIVING TO DIE
CARNAL CHRISTIAN
(Wilderness Living)

BODY
(TEMPLE OF THE HOLY SPIRIT)

SOUL
(PERSONALITY)

Mind
(DECEIVED)

NEW
SPIRIT
(2 COR. 5:17)

Emotions
(VACILLATING)

Will
(FREED BUT YIELDED TO SIN)
ROM. 6:13a

Sin

This illustration is similar to that of the self-centered life shown in chapter 2, except that it is more generic. Those who have not had the psychological difficulties in the earlier diagram may more easily identify with this one. While a person may be psychologically well adjusted, he may be living in defeat spiritually. Attempting to live the Christian life in one's own strength is bound to fail since the flesh is in conflict with the Spirit (Gal. 5:17). The end result of this life is one that produces the works of the flesh (Gal. 5:19-21).

The diagram shown below is similar to the one in chapter 2 that depicts the Christ-centered life. Here we can see that the Holy Spirit, who lives within the spirit of the believer, is controlling the personality and thus the behavior, producing the fruit of the Spirit (Gal. 5:22-23). Or we might say that it is an identity of *being* in order to *do*.

DIAGRAM 15

DYING TO LIVE
SPIRITUAL CHRISTIAN
(Canaan Living)

The diagram can be used to assess your own spiritual journey or to help another do the same on the next page.

At the beginning, we see that a person experiences the new birth and begins to live the Christian life—or attempts to do so. Some who are dealt with deeply by the Holy Spirit begin to live out of Christ's life immediately (A and B occurring simultaneously), which would place them on the upper track, living out of the spiritual identity as

DIAGRAM 16

THE LAW OF THE SPIRIT OF LIFE IN CHRIST JESUS

depicted by the diagram above. This means that such a believer is living out of his resources in Christ, having understood and/or experienced co-death and co-resurrection with Christ, sometimes known as Canaan living (see diagram 12 on page 55).

However, most will follow the bottom track. This track represents the fleshly identity; that is, living out of one's own resources (see diagram 5 on page 31) and asking for God's help to live a good Christian life for several or many years before coming to the place where the Cross is a revealed reality. Looking at the two opposing identities in this manner, it is possible to see that the way to victory is to exchange the fleshly identity for the spiritual identity at the Cross. As we stated before, as soon as a person placed his faith in the Lord Jesus Christ for salvation, the Cross for the Lord Jesus became the Cross for the believer. However, most believers understand only the first aspect of the Cross, that the Lord Jesus died for our sins, and may never experience the liberating truth that they also died and rose with him.

Diagram 9 in chapter 2 shows how the believer is identified with the Lord Jesus the moment he is saved or regenerated. However, he may never appropriate the results of that identification while on planet Earth. This appropriation is a faith transaction similar to that of salvation. While the lost person must recognize and admit that he is a sinner before he sees the need of a Savior, the Christian who is living after the flesh (the bottom track) must likewise sense a great need. The Holy Spirit brings the sinner to a place of conviction about his sinful condition; the selfer (one living after the flesh) must realize the destitute condition of his flesh or of living in his own strength. Brokenness is a vital part of such a realization, and suffering is usually a vital ingredient (Phil. 1:29-30). As the Cross becomes a revealed reality, *it is absolutely amazing the things that death will cure!*

At the time of the exchange, there is generally a prayer of appropriation or relinquishment, at which time the Holy Spirit takes control of the life. At other times, the Holy Spirit does a sovereign work, and prayer takes the form of exaltation and exultation afterward.

When this diagram is viewed as a journey, it becomes, in essence, being led of the Spirit from point A to point B. Along the way, the two identities are brought increasingly into focus, such that one can be exchanged for the other in a faith transaction that is honored by the Holy Spirit. Of course, the shortest distance between two points is a straight line, but the flesh being what it is, there are many deviations as the struggle between the flesh and the Spirit is played out in real life. As the end approaches, there is frequently an intensifying of the conflict, sometimes to such a degree that one may despair even of life. Of course, this is exactly what is happening, in the sense that life as we have known it is being brought to a close—losing our life in order to save it, as described in chapter 5.

Once the death/resurrection process has culminated in the faith transaction, another process begins. Before this, it might be viewed as the negative part of sanctification in which there is a stripping away of the strength of the flesh, which brings the believer to the Cross in his experience. Afterward, there is the positive aspect of sanctification, in which the believer learns to walk in the Spirit (Gal. 5:16) or begins to abide in Christ (John 15:5). This is a lifelong process, during which a person encounters spiritual warfare and the flesh must daily be brought to nothing (Luke 9:23; 2 Cor. 4:11). At times, the flesh assumes the ascendancy again, which means defeat, or what I refer to as a "downer." By this I mean that in the believer's experience, victory has been lost. In the following chapter we will look at how to deal with such downers.

SEVEN

The Anatomy of a Downer and the Way Back to Victory

Up to this point, we have emphasized the path to the cross of Christ and the victory that comes through appropriating our death and resurrection with Christ. Indeed, this is the primary purpose of the book. However, since we have mentioned little regarding the walk afterward, some may think that the Cross is a onetime event, with no defeat or episodes of sin afterward.

So far we have placed comparatively little emphasis on our regaining and maintaining victory. Surely it will be lost from time to time. So it is vital, then, that we discuss the overall process of losing, regaining, and maintaining victory.

Diagram 13 in chapter 5 shows hills and valleys after the appropriation of the Cross in the life of the believer. Immediately after the cross is a peak, indicating victory, followed by a valley showing defeat, that is, a return to the self life or a walk after the flesh. This is what we refer to as a "downer." The believer's experience at this point corresponds directly to the manner in which his flesh has been programmed in his developmental years and in his previous Christian walk. Those who had some fairly severe emotional disturbances may experience regression to a measure of this. Others may be fairly well adjusted and merely experience a loss of power in their lives and witness. Still others may become ensnared again in a particular besetting sin. Usually the defeat will not be of the magnitude known before the experience of victory. But some have regressed to emotional, thought, and behavior patterns similar to those that typified their previous fleshly walk. It is imperative that we take into account the fact that the flesh (self) can never be improved—even after the Cross has become a reality in the life of the believer. We make this assertion so that we might appreciate the absolute necessity of the walk in the Spirit, denying ourselves and taking up the cross daily (Luke 9:23), which is the thesis of this chapter.

The Way Down

Having agreed that all of us will experience "downers," we need to look at a profile of such a downer and understand the dynamics involved. The purpose in doing this is twofold. First, such understanding is necessary if we are to recognize how to prevent their recurrence, or at least to minimize them. Second, we need to know how to deal with them once they are upon us.

In describing the progression of a downer, it might help to compare it to an airplane in flight. Airplanes have what is known as a control column, which usually looks like the lower part of the steering wheel of a car. The column controls the attitude of the plane, fore and aft (front to back) and left to right, as well as its altitude. It is important to keep the plane flying straight and level, but it is possible to crash while maintaining a straight and level attitude if there is not sufficient power.

The plane has an instrument called an altimeter, which shows the pilot whether the plane is gaining or losing altitude or is flying at a constant altitude. If the hands of the altimeter begin to move in a counterclockwise direction and the pilot does nothing about it, he is likely to "buy the farm down below"! But if he notices the altimeter and pulls back on the control column while applying additional power, he will regain altitude. Obviously, the sooner he detects his loss of altitude and makes a correction, the less altitude he will lose. But he may decide "I want to do this all by myself." In that event, he could pull back on the control column, and the nose of the airplane would respond and point upward. However, if he applies no additional power, he will stall, and fall out of the sky and "buy the farm" anyway!

In this analogy, the altitude in diagram 17 represents the level of spiritual victory the believer has gained. Or, to refer back to diagram 13 in the closing pages of chapter 5, the altitude gained initially will be the peak after the cross becomes a reality. This altitude, or level of victory given by the Holy Spirit, may remain somewhat constant for a period of time and then begin to wane. However, the believer has been seated in the heavenlies with his head in the clouds and does not have the benefit of a spiritual "altimeter" to warn him of the fact that he is about to "crash and burn." He may be so taken up with the joy of victory for the first time in his Christian experience that he is all but oblivious to the impending dangers of the world, the flesh, and the devil. As a result, he comes back to earth with a thud and sadly faces again what he had always accepted as reality. If he has not been warned that this is "par for the course," he may begin to run another pity party and return to fleshly living for a while. If and when this does occur, it is necessary to find victory again, just as before, by being always "delivered unto death for Jesus' sake, that the life of Jesus might be made manifest in our mortal flesh" (2 Cor. 4:11).

Since the beginning of the "downer" is one of the most deceptive aspects of the overall process, we will focus on it first. The five steps

DIAGRAM 17
PROFILE OF A DOWNER

at the left of diagram 17 indicate the progression of the "downer," the first stage of which may be very subtle. The more subtle the first stages are, the less likely we are to have a spiritual "altimeter" sensitive enough to detect them. If we do not, one step will lead to another until we are back in the familiar haunts of the flesh without having the foggiest idea of how we got there.

In the gradual (or sudden) descent back to the lower regions of the flesh, I have arbitrarily taken five markers that could and should alert us to impending trouble. However, we can be so anesthetized by the headiness of victory that we go into a spiritual vertigo after the Cross, just as some do prior to the Cross. As you read the markers, which are fairly common, you may choose to engage in some healthy introspection under the guidance of the Holy Spirit to determine where the sequence would start in your own life—perhaps with something such as "Pride goeth before destruction, and an haughty spirit before a fall" (Prov. 16:18). In other words, the first thing might be as simple as pride. In fact, if we define pride as independence, or not abiding in Christ moment by moment, it would be the first step in the sequence of failure for each of us.

For a typical example, we will make #1 something as simple as negative thoughts. Once you are into this, #2 might be the monster called worry. After you have worried, unhindered by the work of the Holy Spirit for a while, there could be some frustration (#3) and the decision to take matters into your own hands. When this happens, you have just hit bottom again. That seems rather simple, but since you have always been in control of things, it is not a giant step to pick up where you left off. Also, since this may have worked fairly well for you in the past, you may be into it for a spell before you realize that your fleshly pattern of living is once more predominant.

Consider next a pattern that may not be quite so subtle but is just as difficult to discern in the beginning if someone has been addicted to this particular profile of operating in the flesh. First, there might be a significant rejection, though it may appear trivial to an onlooker. Next might be the loss of self-esteem, resulting in frustration (#3). If the frustration remains unresolved, it will result in hostility (#4). If the hostility is internalized, it can lead to varying degrees of depression (#5). The result is a deep crisis—another crash. Some may skip depression (#5) and crash at that point by taking their hostility out on someone else verbally, physically, or both.

Obviously, there are as many patterns to the reassertion of the flesh as there are people. But it may help to see that the pattern is always progressive, though the sequence may be more difficult to identify in some people than in others. The point is that understanding your own particular sequence gives you a "spiritual altimeter" to enable you to assess your advance or decline in your spiritual journey. This altimeter may be "red-lined" for one or more danger points. Even if you happen to be soaring in victory and gaining spiritual altitude, there are dangers aplenty. When you are in victory, you are on the cutting edge for the Lord and have been promoted to the front lines. And when you are on the front lines, you are very likely to get some direct attacks from the enemy of our souls, the devil. Ignorance of the devil's devices can be just as devastating as being deceived or unaware of the subtle encroachment of the flesh.

On the other hand, the emotional component in victory can be so new and intoxicating that some people may ride their emotions into an orbit that is more fleshly than spiritual. Taken in this sense, an "upper" could be just as deceiving as a "downer." Since an "upper" usually does not cause as much consternation as a "downer," we have not depicted it on the diagram. The point of all this is that the earlier we detect the decline, which is more general than the incline, or "upper," the less the loss of spiritual altitude we will experience.

In the beginning of the journey of learning to walk in the Spirit (Gal. 5:16), it is common for the believer to be in the midst of a downer before he is aware that he is losing spiritual altitude. It is just second nature (flesh) for the believer to revert to type and do things the way he has always done them, particularly when he is well into adulthood before he experiences victory for the first time. Often the believer may almost despair since he may think his experience with the Lord was unreal or faulty or that he can never regain victory once he has lost it. Not a few have thought that it was impossible for them ever to be defeated again, and when they were, it caused great disillusionment.

If you happen to find yourself in your first downer or your fifteenth or your fiftieth, I would challenge you to go back, retrace your steps, and determine what was the first event that precipitated your downward slide. Ask the Holy Spirit to help you in determining the sequence in this particular downer, and you may gain some clues about a pattern that is typical for you. Then you can use these as red flags to alert you that a crash situation is imminent unless you take corrective action.

As in the airplane analogy, it is necessary to lay hold of the control column, the Cross, and apply power—the Holy Spirit's power—if you are to regain spiritual altitude. Obviously, the earlier you do this the less altitude you will lose. If we deal with the spiritual decline at its inception, *we* will know it; if we wait to deal with it at the bottom, *everyone* may know it. It is not absolutely necessary to hit the bottom every time, but whether you crash or pay heed to your spiritual altimeter and deal with the decline in its early stages, the answer is the same. However, many of us want to lay hold of the control column in our own strength and mechanically (intellectually) go through the procedure. If we do, we will find that the flesh does not cause us to regain altitude. On the contrary, just the opposite occurs. We fail and fall again. It is only in the power of the Holy Spirit that we will find victory. And it is in the power of the Holy Spirit that we regain and maintain a victorious walk: "This I say then, Walk in the Spirit, and ye shall not fulfil the lust of the flesh" (Gal. 5:16).

The Way Up

To illustrate the dynamics of deliverance from a downer, we return to diagram 9 from chapter 2 to see two truths about redemption—the cross and the blood of Christ. In one sense, the two cannot be separated, since both occurred simultaneously and both are vital to the finished work of Calvary. However, the Bible ascribes some of our blessings to the Cross and others to the blood.

From my experience, it seems that the blood deals with what we *do* while the Cross deals with what we *are*. While this seems to be true, I realized while reading the verse below that I haven't given enough emphasis to the work of the blood of Christ in my life and ministry.

> Of how much sorer punishment, suppose ye, shall he be thought worthy, who hath trodden under foot the Son of God, and hath counted the blood of the covenant, wherewith he was sanctified, an unholy thing, and hath done despite unto the Spirit of grace? (Heb. 10:29)

After I read that portion of Scripture, I began a study of Hebrews, especially chapters 8 through 10. Though my study isn't finished, some truths have emerged that have helped me understand how we maintain victory and find a way up from our downers.

You will note that diagram 18 (page 102) contains an important addition: The segment to the right joins us, in our walk here below, to our Lord, in whom we are seated in the heavenlies (Eph. 2:6). We must understand the benefits of being seated in him before we are to walk in victory and be able to stand against the wiles of the enemy.

Since our walk in the Spirit is a moment-by-moment appropriation of the power of the Holy Spirit, or denying ourselves and taking up the cross daily (Luke 9:23), and since we are sanctified by the blood (Heb. 10:29), it is vital that we see the flow of power to and through us if we are to maintain our victory in him. This continuous flow is depicted by the direction of the arrows in the figure 8 on its side in the diagram. As you can see, the cross, the blood, and the Spirit of God are all indispensable agents as the life of the Lord Jesus Christ is being lived out through us.

The tabernacle God instructed Moses to build had three parts: the outer court, the Holy Place, and the Holy of Holies. The blood was prominent in all three of these places. Many Christians remain outer-court Christians, who know that the blood has dealt with the penalty or guilt of sin. Others enter into the Holy Place and become involved in their worship and service and see the blood as the basis of the forgiveness of sins. Then there are those who have denied themselves and taken up their Cross and have entered into fellowship in the Holy of Holies, trusting in the blood to overcome the power of sin in their lives. Though all these redemptive works of God on our behalf were accomplished simultaneously at Calvary, each must be applied separately in our ongoing walk.

DIAGRAM 18

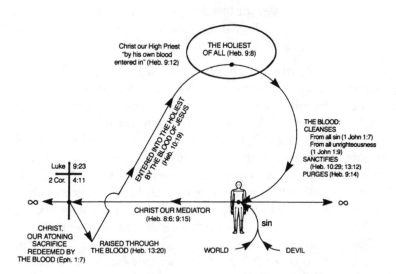

It is much easier for our finite minds to grasp the function of the historical blood of Christ poured out at Calvary for our sins than it is to understand the work of his blood in our lives today in purging our "conscience from dead works" (Heb. 9:14) and sprinkling our hearts from an "evil conscience" (Heb. 10:22). Perhaps this is the reason we hear less teaching on the latter and are not more consistently buoyed up out of our downers by the power of the blood of Christ.

The verses shown at certain junctures are important and should be studied as you move along through the flow of power in the diagram. In chapter 2, diagram 9 shows the believer's position in Christ as seated in the heavenlies, victorious over the world, the flesh, and the devil. As we enter into the reality of that vital truth, not only has the cross of Christ been efficacious in our lives but so has the blood. However, we may not be aware of the place of the blood of Christ in the victory given by the Holy Spirit.

At the Cross the Lord Jesus Christ was the sacrificial Lamb whose blood was shed for all mankind. He had paid the price for the guilt of sin, and redemption was complete. That is how on the cross he could declare, "It is finished." In heaven, he is our High Priest, or minister, of the new sanctuary where he has done all that is necessary to cover our sins. In us here on earth, he is our life (Col. 3:3) and our mediator (Heb. 8:6; 9:15). As our mediator, he undertakes to assure that we will keep our end of the bargain, so to speak. Therefore, we can be just as certain that he will do his work in our hearts as we are that he has already done the work in heaven.

As believers, we have appropriated the truth that the blood of the Lord Jesus was shed for our sins: "And that he was buried, and that he rose again the third day according to the scriptures" (1 Cor. 15:4). However, we may not be as familiar with this truth: "Now the God of peace, that brought again from the dead our Lord Jesus, that great shepherd of the sheep, through the blood of the everlasting covenant, make you perfect in every good work" (Heb. 13:20-21). It was through the blood that Christ was raised to new life.

Then it was "by his own blood he entered in once into the holy place, having obtained eternal redemption for us" (Heb. 9:12). It is, likewise, our birthright "to enter into the holiest by the blood of Jesus" (Heb. 10:19). However, our "entering into the holiest" is contingent upon our flesh having been dealt with by the cross of Christ. We read: "Having therefore, brethren, boldness to enter into the holiest by the blood of Jesus, by a new and living way, which he hath consecrated for us, through the veil, that is to say, his flesh" (Heb. 10:19-20). His physical flesh had to be rent for him "to enter into the holiest," and our veil, which is the flesh, or self, prevents us from entering into intimate fellowship with him. Although the veil in the temple was rent from top to bottom and the way for unhindered and unbroken fellowship was made possible, we yet have a veil of our own making, the flesh, which must continuously be dealt with by the cross and the blood of Christ. Once the Holy Spirit has illuminated the truth of our death and resurrection with Christ and it is an experiential reality, we must continue to "deny ourselves and take up our cross daily."

Then, as we "enter into the holiest by the blood of Jesus" (Heb. 10:19) and by faith appropriate the truth that we are seated in the heavenlies (Eph. 2:6), we can also appropriate the work of the blood of Christ in our lives here on earth. It is necessary that we deal continuously with the defilement of sin. By confession, we are acknowledging our need for the continuous cleansing power of the blood in our lives moment by moment. As we confess our sins (1 John 1:9) and "walk in the light, as he is in the light, we have fellowship one with another, and the blood of Jesus Christ his Son cleanseth us from all sin" (1 John 1:7). However, it is easier to understand that we are forgiven on the basis of the shed blood of Christ than it is to understand how we are, within ourselves, cleansed from all sin and from all unrighteousness.

But the work of the blood of Christ in our lives goes on beyond cleansing us from what we have done. We are sanctified through his blood (Heb. 10:29; 13:12). We have "hearts sprinkled from an evil conscience" (Heb. 10:22), and our consciences may be purged from dead works that we may serve the living God (Heb. 9:14). It is the cross of Christ that deals with what we are (or, better, *were*). But it is the blood that deals with what we do and what caused us to do it—the power of indwelling sin. It is impossible to ascribe too much power to the blood, even though our finite minds will never lay hold of all that is available through the blood of Christ as the Holy Spirit ministers it to our point of greatest need.

As you will note in diagram 18, the arrows show a continuous flow of power. In fact, you might imagine the arrows as continually moving around the figure-eight pattern in the direction they are pointing. As we move along through life here on earth, it is a continuous process of denying ourselves, taking up the cross daily, taking our place by faith in the heavenlies, confessing known sin, being cleansed from all unrighteousness, and having our conscience purged from dead works. Taken together, these constitute the life known as abiding or fellowship or walking in the Spirit.

If we fail to "yield [ourselves] to God, as those that are alive from the dead, and [our] members as instruments of righteousness unto God," we will do the converse and "yield [our] members as instruments of unrighteousness unto sin" (Rom. 6:13). Or to put it another way, we yield either to the working of the blood in our lives or to the power of sin. As we have seen, it is the Spirit, working through the blood of Christ, that is our source of continuous victory. The diagram depicts this option—yielding to the power of sin or to the power of the blood as applied to our lives by the Holy Spirit.

If we yield to sin, we walk according to the flesh, and the power of the blood of Christ is circumvented or short-circuited. It is not that the blood is no longer efficacious but that we have failed to count or reckon upon it. In ignorance we may yield to sin's deception and walk according to the flesh while trying desperately to serve God. If so, we are in a downer and may not even know it. Once we are alerted to our plight by our own unique "spiritual altimeter," we must deal not only with *sins* but also with *sin*. We must confess the sins, but we must also deal with sin by reckoning ourselves dead to it (Rom. 6:11; Luke 9:23, 2 Cor. 4:11) and by opening ourselves by faith to the cleansing, sanctifying, purging, and sprinkling of the blood of Christ. As we do, we find the Holy Spirit restoring us to the place of victory over the world, the flesh, and the devil. To put it back into the parlance we have been using, we have regained our "spiritual altitude" to where we are again abiding in our risen Lord.

As we by faith abide in the finished work of the Cross, the present work of the Spirit, and the blood of Christ, it is our birthright to "produce much fruit" (John 15:5). Downers will come and downers will go, but the blood never loses its power to cleanse and restore, that all glory may go to God for what he has done.

The Precious Blood

God's Word is filled with Blood
From beginning to the end—
From that of Abel's sacrifice (Gen. 4:4)
Until God his Son did send (Rom. 5:8).
In Heaven, too, its work was done (Heb. 9:22)
By Jesus, our High Priest;
In Revelation John declares,
Its power has never ceased (Rev. 12:11).

In our finite way of thinking,
We are most concerned with sins,
And confess them all we must (1 John 1:9)
That Calv'ry our pardon wins.
But there is a deeper meaning
As many of us are sensing;
It goes beyond forgiveness
That, too, we might know cleansing.

Redemption has many facets,
But at Calvary it was finished (John 19:30);
Though his Blood was shed but once (Heb. 10:12, 14),
Its power is undiminished.
Through its power our Lord was raised (Heb. 13:20)
And to his Father did ascend:
His body broken at the Cross (1 Pet. 2:24)
And the temple's veil did rend (Matt. 27:51).

By his own Blood he entered (Heb. 9:12)
Once for all the Holy Place;
He op'ed the Fount of Blessing—
Bids us to the Throne of Grace (Heb. 4:16).
His Blood is our only merit (Heb. 4:16)
As we would his bidding do;

Our access to the Holy Place
Means our flesh we must eschew (Luke 9:23).

In that blessed Holy Place (Eph. 1:3)
Our life's hid with Christ in God (Col. 3:3);
Our High Priest he can be
Because he has, likewise, trod (Heb. 4:15).
And, so, the work in Heaven
Leaves nothing to be done,
But for us to act in faith
On the victory he has won!

As we walk with him in Light (1 John 1:7)
His Blood cleanses from all sin;
With others we have fellowship (1 John 1:3)
As the Savior reigns within.
Cleansed from all unrighteousness (1 John 1:9)
As in Christ Jesus we abide, (John 15:5)
His Blood not only cleanses;
But by it we're sanctified! (Heb. 10:29; 13:12).

We can know all sins are gone
And, yet, be conscience smitten;
But, again, the Blood's the answer
As in the Book 'tis written:
How much more the Blood of Christ
Through the eternal Spirit offered
Purge your conscience from dead works (Heb. 9:14)—
The promise which is proffered.

The Blood sufficed in Heaven
Our sins with which to deal;
The Holy Spirit lacks no power
Our sin wounds here to heal.
Our High Priest did in Heav'n

What our Mediator does on Earth (Heb. 8:6; 9:15);
Our sins completely covered there—
He assures us here our worth.

Oh, the precious Blood of Jesus
God imbued with matchless power;
That we, his sons, need not let
Sin's reign to cause us cower.
When the devil would come in
And deluge us like a flood (Isa. 59:19),
We have only to remind him
He was conquered by the Blood.

And now, my friend, I bid you
To consider the above;
Allow the Spirit to teach you
About the Fountain of his love.
His Blood covers and cleanses—
Flowing from his riven side,
But is only fraught with power
As in Christ Jesus we abide (John 15:5).

When we fail to give the Blood
Its place in our lives today,
We've all but trodden under foot (Heb. 10:29)
The power that fills our way.
But God in sovereign grace
Continues to draw us ever;
Our lives redeemed by Precious Blood
From him can nothing sever! (Rom. 8:38-39).

Because redemption is complete
We and our Lord know union;
'Tis in the blessed Holy Place
That we can know communion.

When we cease from our own works (Heb. 4:9-11)
In him we are truly blessed;
And rejoice to do his bidding—
"Come unto me and rest" (Matt. 11:28).

C. R. Solomon

EIGHT

Testimonies of GFI— God's Faithful Intervention

The following are just a few testimonies of what God has done over the years through the ministry of Grace Fellowship International. Five of the eight first-person testimonies are from members of the helping professions, whose lives have been changed and who have integrated their faith and their practice. It is not our desire to honor the counselor(s) involved but rather to give glory to God for the changes the Holy Spirit has wrought and for how these people have gone on to share these truths and see God use them in the same way. The other testimonies have been summarized without giving enough detail to identify the persons involved while still stating the case accurately.

> I was born in South Africa, educated in England, and worked as a professional psychologist, lecturer, and management consultant in several European countries. On June 15, 1995, I testified to a large audience how, at the age of fifty-five, I found victory in the Lord Jesus Christ from a lifelong struggle with depression. During most of those preceding years I practiced and taught psychology, proclaiming the hope of a permanent solution to depression within the methods and therapies of my profession. The paradox was that I could not cure myself. The "solutions" were only temporary and short lived before the symptoms would engulf me again, dragging me back to square one.

This self-defeating cycle became the pattern of my inner personal life as I tried to hide the condition from the world around me. I saw a similar pattern in the struggles of depressed clients as they entered and returned through the revolving doors of the clinic.

Eventually I left the clinical setting to specialize in educational psychology and, later on, in organizational behavior. (This discipline is known as industrial psychology in the USA or occupational psychology in the UK). This specialization gave me entry into the world of corporate giants and entrepreneurial executives in large multinational organizations. Large chunks of responsibility and financial resources were given to psychologists who had this expertise, in order to develop resource strategies and training programs in leadership, cross-cultural team building, motivation, creative thinking, and interpersonal effectiveness.

Many years spent in this field brought an awareness of the self-imposed stress built into such programs, where characteristics of independence, individuality, self-assertiveness, and personal power were upheld in a competitive and predominantly male environment. Here again, the focus was on strengthening the "self," leading to a narcissistic preoccupation with the self that, paradoxically, brought about further stress. This observation was confirmed by the popularity of seminars on stress and conflict management, where countless testimonies of self-defeat, despair, and depression came to the surface.

My depression became larger than life and increasingly difficult to conceal. The self-deception was finally exposed when, in a car accident in January 1990, I was instantaneously stripped of all my worldly sources of significance: my position, status, professional expertise, and other indicators of success. Brain injuries caused permanent damage to some speech, intellectual, and motor functioning, leaving me unable to continue my career and privileged lifestyle.

The self was dethroned. While in a semivegetable state in

intensive care, the Lord brought me to the foot of his Cross. My whole life flashed before my "inner" eyes. The words of Isaiah 30:18-22 penetrated the scarred tissue of what was left of my memory as the strongholds of pride and idolatry began to crumble. The Spirit of God pushed me to the margins of my individuality. My preoccupation with my own importance had to go so that my inner personality could be reconciled in fellowship with God, in humble identification with the Cross and the resurrected life of Christ Jesus in me (Gal. 2:20). Over a period of three years the Lord restored part of the brain damage, drawing me closer into a totally dependent relationship with him. As he became more and more the center of my life, I experienced the words of Isaiah 30:26 and a lasting freedom from depression, despite some remaining physical and intellectual disabilities.

So five years later as I stood in front of that audience, I felt compelled to revisit the psychology of depression with these experiences of biblical truths and the newfound power of the Christ life in me. It took another year before the Lord sent me Charles Solomon's *Handbook to Happiness* through an interim pastor's wife at our church in Brussels, Belgium, where I now live. While reading it in one sitting, everything I had experienced became crystal clear to me and fell into place: Here at last was a conceptual framework within which to reconcile the major psychological themes and explanations with biblical solutions! Since then, I have found Dr. Solomon's *Wheel and Line in Spirituotherapy* to be a powerful tool, mightily used by the Holy Spirit, not only in the counseling room but also in training seminars.

Annette Myburgh
Brussels, Belgium

I have been a most blessed person. I was born into a loving Christian home and came to a saving knowledge of Jesus Christ at age eleven. I surrendered to full-time ministry at age seventeen and have followed that commitment faithfully through ten years of student work and nineteen years as a pastor.

Although I was blessed and well educated through college and seminary, I was struggling in my personal spiritual life with a "fear of failure." This caused tension in my life and family, which, in turn, caused me to "redouble my efforts" and "perform" even harder! Everything appeared balanced in my life, but internally the "battle was on"! This war continued through a brief stay in the hospital (from fatigue and tension) and through ten years of student work.

During this decade, when I was between thirty and forty years of age, God was preparing me for my death to "self" and my personal understanding and experience of the identification truths found in Romans 6, 7, and 8. I was hungry for that "deeper life" and personal victory expressed in 2 Corinthians 5:17 and Galatians 2:20. I began studying the Deeper Life writers and pursuing the identification truths, when it became plain to me that life-transforming ministry could not happen apart from the centrality of the Cross. Everything I was studying led me forward until I read Dr. Charles Solomon's book *Handbook to Happiness*. It was then that I knew I had found the secret to the Christ- and Cross-centered life. In 1980, at the age of forty, I attended the three-day conference and five-day workshop in Denver, Colorado.

That is when things really began to happen in my life, my family, and my ministry. Since then, I have been committed to teaching these life-giving truths. This teaching has focused my life, transformed my family and ministry, and taught me how to answer the deepest needs of people while establishing them in the faith as they grow to maturity, realizing the "fullness of Christ" as he is formed within them. This is truly freedom in Christ by way of the Cross! And it is the only real answer!

Rev. Stoney Shaw
St. Louis, Missouri

I was born in 1925, the second of three boys, and found myself in a hurting family. My older brother was severely physically handicapped due to birth trauma. The younger one was also traumatized during the birth process, and my mother had her hands, heart, and time filled with the care of these two very needy children.

It was not too long before I found myself emotionally very much alone. My mother was understandably devoted to the two children with limited abilities. She loved me, too, but had little time to demonstrate it. She was, as I look back now, a wonderful Christian. She often prayed in her bedroom with the door open, and I heard her! As my life, in sheer rebellion against what I perceived to be neglect, became more troublesome to her, I heard her fervent prayers.

My father, a dear man of God, would come home to a wife devoted to the less fortunate, and therefore she had little "energy" for him. Father was motivated to do "well," and he became a very "successful" businessman. He performed well and, by example, taught me to do the same.

By the time I was a teenager, I had seen the negative aspects of life. My father, though successful, was a very unhappy man. His Christianity did not bring the inner peace he was looking for. I was taken to church and Sunday school. I learned to perform better than anyone else; I jumped through all the "hoops." I was praised, but I was empty, shy, withdrawn. But life had to go on.

Medical school was next (that had been my father's desire for himself). By graduation my thoughts were: *If I can do this, anyone can!* But it felt so good to be called "Dr. Kaschel"! Then the novelty wore off, as it always does in the world. What could I do for an encore? Of course! Become a specialist—a psychiatrist!

I was married by this time, and we had four children. To anyone looking on, life seemed OK. But inwardly I was miserable, depressed, looking for an honorable way OUT! Bridge abutments were tempting, but with my fortune, even hitting one at 80 mph would only cripple me and make matters worse! I felt no one cared. Certainly God was not real—if he even existed. He hadn't helped me.

About that time my mother's prayers were coming before the throne of God! God "dropped the other shoe!" Life fell apart. I was desperate. Into my life walked Dr. Solomon—mind you, an Ed.D. What could I, a medical director of a psychiatric hospital, learn from him? I was to find that God works in mysterious ways. After hearing this Dr. Solomon, I had to admit, "You have *an* answer; I have none."

It took about four months, further misery, attempts at self-help, etc., before I was willing to talk further. We then met in Denver. I saw lives changed, radically, as I sat in on counseling sessions.

"How can you guys do this?" I wondered. "I'll pay you if you teach me this method."

"You have to come to the Cross!"

I began to hear that until I wanted to scream!

God was at work in me. I screamed. I kicked. I negotiated. I promised. I wept. God would *not* listen! Finally, the convicting power of the Holy Spirit brought me to the "end." I let him strip me of all I had built up as a defense. I began to soar. New life in Christ became my possession, my life, through the Cross—not only forgiveness, but a new life!

My whole approach to people has changed. Whereas I had a psychiatric practice, I now minister Christ. I, too, see lives radically changed. Later, the Lord opened the opportunity to go to Europe for eleven years and minister the truths God had taught me. Between trips overseas, my private counseling office remained fully scheduled. Many were people who had "seen all Job's friends," and "nothing got better, only worse." Insurance benefits were gone. To see people at that extremity often led to the blessing of life changes, family restoration, and an inner peace they had never experienced before. The change has been more than a "renewal"; it has been a "new life" for me. God is so worthy of my praise!

Paul Kaschel
Grand Rapids, Michigan

I was supposedly "saved" when I was five years old. I answered all of the questions of a pastor from a major denominational church correctly and prayed the sinner's prayer verbatim. However, I knew nothing of spiritual things.

At twenty-five, with a wife and three children, my daily consumption of alcohol was out of control. It was then that I trusted Jesus as Lord, Savior, and Life. My conversion experience entailed a conscious understanding of my "self" somehow being put aside and Jesus Christ becoming my very life. This was my first experience with the cross of Christ and identifying with Jesus as Life. At this point in my life, I felt the call of God into ministry, but because of fear of failure and lack of faith, I would not surrender to that call.

No one in the church could explain what had happened apart from a dramatic salvation experience. It was obvious that Jesus was living his life through me. This prompted the church leaders to overload me with responsibilities far beyond my spiritual maturity. I bought into the denominational philosophy that I must somehow "keep the Holy Spirit and really begin to work for God."

Thus began my tragic regression into a walk after the flesh.

After twelve years of living hell, the Cross again became a reality in my life.

"Not I, but Christ" was again my heart's cry. This time, through the writings of Dr. Solomon and others, I had more understanding of how the faith life was to be lived.

Armed with only an associate degree at the time, my wife and I answered the Lord's call on our lives to begin a Christian counseling center. After an internship in Denver, Colorado, with Dr. Solomon, we returned to Texas and began to counsel Christians, applying the truth of the exchanged life to every situation. The results have been nothing short of miraculous. Problems such as marital infidelity, divorce, child molestation (both victim and abuser), drug and alcohol addiction, suicidal depression, mania, parent-child conflict, and demonic oppression are commonly seen and successfully resolved.

The truth of Galatians 2:20, "not I, but Christ," transforms lives on a daily basis. *Handbook to Happiness* is given to every client after the first visit.

Jesus Christ promised that the eternal Holy Spirit of God will be our counselor if we accept our death, burial, resurrection, and life with him.

He cannot lie.

J. Maxwell
Tyler, Texas

On January 1, 1993, I went into our study for my "special quiet time" on New Year's Day. I say "special quiet time" because it has been my habit to always spend the first part of my day with him, but on New Year's Day I dedicate more time and attention to this day of new beginnings. I also write in my prayer journal on these occasions so I can look back and see the work of God in my life and the life of my family. At this point of my career as a geophysicist for an oil company, times were very uncertain, as is so often the case in this business. I sensed God speaking to me about this. In my journal I wrote: "Lord . . . you have brought to my attention Ephesians 5:15, "Be very careful, then, how you live—not as unwise but as wise, making the most of every opportunity because the days are evil" (NIV). I had underlined "making the most of every opportunity," knowing God was going to give us some kind of opportunity in 1993. I also wrote in the journal three prayers of "resolution": (1) to be delivered from the stronghold of fear; (2) to be delivered from a critical attitude, to be an encourager; and (3) to be delivered from "the love of money." At forty-three, the time was ripe for God to do some major reconstruction and healing in my life.

He did not waste any time. Within six weeks of those prayers I was laid off from my employer of twelve years—the first layoff in my twenty years of work. For any man, this is a very difficult event, but for a man with a stronghold of fear it was devastating. I got laid off on a Monday, and the following Friday some friends let us borrow their lake-house getaway for some intense time to seek the Lord. Denise and I just took some clothes and our Bibles and for twenty-four hours did nothing but read the Word, pray, share, and sleep. It was the most concentrated time of prayer we had ever had. God reminded us of the story told in 2 Kings 4:1-7 about the widow and the jars of oil. One truth he showed us was how we must be empty vessels for him to be able to fill us with his oil, the Holy Spirit.

A few days later I was speaking to a pastor friend about my situation and how I wasn't sure if I was supposed to stay in the oil business or if God wanted me to change careers. I had been a lay counselor at our church, Second Baptist, for years and was seeking the Lord's guidance about pursuing a counseling career. This friend had attended an Exchanged Life seminar recently and suggested I attend one that was coming up in about a week. I signed up and attended this four-day event, really listening but at the end not really "getting the full picture." I was supposed to have read *Handbook to Happiness* before the conference but never got to it. The conference ended on a Saturday at noon, and the following Monday I had to take a business trip for a small one-day consulting job I had received from a Christian friend. On the plane I began reading the book, and the longer I read, the clearer the picture became. The reality and truth of the need to "go to the cross" was really beginning to sink in.

Finally it got so intense, I had to close the book and put it under my seat! I knew God was saying something very powerful and important, and I did not want to go there, especially on a plane full of people. This was something I needed to approach alone. That evening in my motel room I fearfully pulled out the book again and finished reading it, confirming where God was taking me. On March 11, 1993, I got on my knees and prayed the selfer's prayer, not long after feeling like the guy rolling down the hospital hall to surgery that would save his life but dreading the "cost" of pain and suffering he would have to go through. It was a very special moment that I will always remember—and my life has not been the same since.

David Glenn
Houston, Texas

While a student in seminary, I pastored a church that had grown greatly in numbers and different ministries during the two years that I was there. The minister of music, meaning well, brought forth a startling revelation to me on my last Sunday there. He said, "We are going to dedicate this song, 'How Great Thou Art,' to Rev. Larry Renetzky." The Holy Spirit really convicted me. Here I thought Christ was being lifted up and the Father glorified, but I got in the way and was given the credit.

For twelve years I searched for an answer. Finally, God answered my prayers. Truly his word "seek, and ye shall find" (Matt. 7:7, 18) came alive for me. A dear brother in Christ introduced me to Dr. Solomon through his book *Handbook to Happiness* around 1974, and finally in person in 1976. "Know the truth, and the truth shall make you free" (John 8:32) was revealed to me in the context of Galatians 2:20, and the exchanged life came alive for me. I was a good, sincere, and dedicated man in Christian ministry, but I was not a Christ-centered Christian counselor and pastor until the truths of Dr. Solomon's book set me free from my self-centered life.

Today I celebrate my twenty-fifth anniversary of this revelation of the Christ-centered life and praise and thank God for my friend and brother in Christ, Dr. Charles Solomon, and his book *Handbook to Happiness*. Truly his books and his Exchanged Life seminar have transformed my life. I start every day giving up self to be crucified anew with Jesus and pray that I will live more by the faith of the Son of God, who loves me and gave himself for me. I have seen hundreds of individuals, couples, and families transformed through the exchanged life. Truly, the Christ-centered life makes a difference in those with whom I counsel.

It is my hope and prayer that as you read this book, you will exchange your life for the life of Jesus and live to the glory and praise of God the Father through Jesus Christ. You can experience the difference that Jesus can make in you, your marriage, and family when Christ is the center of your life.

Larry Renetzky
Amarillo, Texas

A pedophile had been arrested and had been in psychiatric treatment for molesting young girls. He was also a voyeur and had excessive sexual relations with his wife. When he came for counseling, he was not a Christian and didn't intend to discuss spiritual things. However, he accepted the Lord Jesus Christ in the first interview and subsequently understood his co-death and co-resurrection with Christ.

During his fourth interview three weeks later, the counselor asked, "How are the compulsions regarding young girls?"

He replied, "They are gone."

"What else is different?"

He replied, "Now I see women as something besides sex objects."

His wife had awakened *him* for physical relations the previous night, and his inordinate need was gone.

About a year later, his brother called and asked what we had done to his brother. We answered that the Holy Spirit—not the counselor—had done something. He stated that he and his brother had had a conversation for the first time in their lives—after more than thirty years.

A married man with children also lived in homosexual sin. When a young man threatened to report him, this man sought help by attending a conference on the exchanged life. He found victory during the first day and was set free from homosexuality. About a year later, he brought his wife to another conference, where he was interviewed before the group. As he related the details of his new life, his wife asserted that she truly had a husband for the first time.

A man who had been depressed for eight years was on medication for clinical depression and for headaches; in fact, he was addicted to the headache medication. His psychiatrist was planning to administer ECT (electroconvulsive therapy) if his client didn't improve in two weeks. At the end of the second spiritual counseling interview in two successive days, this man completely abandoned his life to the Lord Jesus Christ and claimed by faith his death and resurrection with Christ. When he returned the next day, he had no depression for the first time in eight years. Almost ten years later, he still had not suffered a significant depression.

A chronic mental patient had been treated by psychologists and psychiatrists for twenty years, both as an outpatient and in many admissions to psychiatric hospitals, some up to seven months in duration, and including ECT and insulin-shock therapy. Her husband said they had spent more than fifty thousand (pre-1970) dollars on medication alone, to say nothing of doctors and hospitals. At age sixteen this woman had found her father dead of a suicide. She had her first breakdown at age eighteen and another at age thirty, when she began the rounds of various approaches to therapy.

The spiritual counselor had seen her three times the previous year, when she had declined further sessions. A year later she called on the phone, and the counselor confronted her very directly with the claims of Christ on her life. At this point this woman was virtually skin and bones, taking eight tranquilizers a day and heavy sleeping medication at night. Then the Holy Spirit released her.

She broke into tears and found victory in Christ that day. Within a month, under medical supervision, she was off tranquilizers and sleeping medication; within three months she had gained seventeen pounds. When her ophthalmologist examined her, he was astounded. It was the first time he had ever seen her when she did not have tension in her eyes.

Although she was a Christian and had been through various types of therapy, including recovery, she had not resolved the internal conflict of a lifetime. She had had multiple abortions and marriages and was experiencing attacks of rage. She and her husband were afraid she was going to harm their child. She had also been addicted to alcohol and drugs but had been dry for several years.

When she came for spiritual counseling and the first interview came to a close, she spontaneously said, "Let's kill me off!" Whereupon the counselor replied, "OK, let's." She knelt and surrendered her life to the Lord Jesus and claimed by faith her death and resurrection with Christ. When she arose from her knees, she was free and had victory in Christ. Her husband reported that he had a "new" wife, and she was still walking in victory almost eight years later.

This Christian man's heart rate was regularly 100 beats per minute and as high as 150 during panic attacks. After completing four or five sessions with the spiritual counselor, he was lying in his bed one night when his pulse suddenly dropped to 70; he thought he was dying! He called his wife to take him to the hospital, and she said, "What are you going to tell the doctor? He will send you to a mental hospital!" As the Holy Spirit dealt with him in the midst of a crisis, some of his other symptoms left at the same time.

One lady had the entire medical community stumped concerning how to treat her physical ailments. She was so weak by the end of each day that she was certain she was going to die. She read *The Ins and Out of Rejection,* and much that she had previously repressed began to surface. Both she and her husband thought she was losing her mind, and she called for an appointment. The counselor explained the way of freedom through the Cross, and she privately decided to allow the Holy Spirit full sway in her life.

One day when she was alone, the Holy Spirit brought to her mind a hurtful event from her past that she had repressed. Once she was able to process it and forgive those involved, she was free of the effects of this particular event and began to feel better physically.

After other such occurrences the Holy Spirit brought the biggest one to her mind. Once she had dealt with it, she was free, and her physical symptoms disappeared. The Holy Spirit seemed to be systematically "downloading" her repressed information to her memory so that she could process it and allow him to deliver her from it. A few years later her older sister visited her and confirmed all of the events that the Holy Spirit had revealed to her.

A missionary lady's emotional problems had had a negative impact on her ministry and that of her husband. They had left the field after almost twenty years, and she came for help.

In eliciting the history, the spiritual counselor had

learned that as the woman was growing up, her father had told her that she was not worth her salt, so, of course, that is the way she felt. The counselor told her, "Your earthly father says that you are not worth your salt; your heavenly Father says you are worth his Son. Now which will be the basis for your identity from this point on—salt or Son?"

She had previously understood her identification with Christ intellectually; now the Holy Spirit made it real experientially. She lost her life based on salt and found her new life based on her being in the Son of God. God transformed her life, and the missionary couple returned to the mission field to complete what they had started.

She was in her early twenties and was anorexic, weighing only sixty pounds when she came for counseling. She found victory in the first interview and had gained ten pounds by the time she came for her third session. When the counselor asked her what she did when she encountered a situation with the loved one who had oriented her toward anorexia, she said, "I just look up and praise the Lord for the negative circumstances and rest in my Lord." Approximately a year later, the counselor attended her wedding.

One woman had planned to take her life by taking a bottle of pills and then throwing herself off a mountain. If the fall didn't kill her, the pills would!

However, she decided to read some of *The Ins and Out of Rejection* before she implemented her plan. She read the statement that suicide was the epitome of self-centeredness, and she couldn't make this fit with her rationale for taking her life. She came off the mountain for a counseling session. She lost her life at the Cross and dealt with the issues that had driven her to the brink of suicide. She wanted to get rid of herself, and she did—in the right way.

The following letter is from an inmate in Florida.

I felt compelled to write you to let you know how much your book *Handbook to Happiness and You*, and the truths contained therein, have set me "free" from my self-struggle. I had been "wrestling" with the flesh instead of "resting in Christ." I truly see where it is impossible to live a victorious Christian life any other way. I was born again in April 1992, but I didn't know, or was not shown, "the Cross" and the work already done there. It has been a roller coaster ride to say the least, but I now know that this battle has already been dealt with by Christ. I was fortunate that Brother Lee Lefebre, of Exchanged Life Ministries, sent me a copy of your splendid spiritual book. I now enjoy the exchanged life myself.

Perry K. Martin
Milton, Florida

God's Processing Tunnel: Charles Solomon's Testimony in Verse

Egypt

As we embark on the journey of life
And partake of its burdens and cares;
Ere long we loathe the turmoil and strife
And seek respite from its snares.

In vain we search for joy that endures
Among the pleasures and trinkets of Earth;
Only to find that which beckons and lures
Is empty and void of true worth.

On and on 'til the restless heart cries
For the relentless ache to cease;
Oh, for Someone to wipe tears from our eyes (Rev. 7:17)
And flood our beings with peace (John 16:33).

At length we see that he who died
Was acquainted with sorrow and grief (Isa. 53:3-4),
And we come, confessing our sin and pride (Rom. 10:9-10, 13)
And in coming, experience relief (John 5:24; 8:32).

Wilderness

In this newfound Friend all grace resides
That abounds to our every need (2 Cor. 9:8);
The promise is to him who in Jesus abides (John 15:5-7),
To him who from Self has been freed.

But the monster Self is a dauntless foe
That insists on ruling the life (Rom. 7:18-19),
So instead of the peace we fain would know,
We encounter a new kind of strife.

As the battle rages and clouds are dark
And our way with heartaches is lined (Rom. 7:24),
We almost give up; we almost give out; when hark—
A promise: "I will bring the blind . . ." (Isa. 42:16).

Many are the doubts as he leads us along
By a path that we would not choose,
But clinging to him, we can't go wrong,
Since our life, to save, we must lose (Luke 9:23-24).

As in a tunnel whose center is black
We yearn for light on our path,
In the wall of despair we search for a crack
That we might walk by sight—not faith (2 Cor. 5:7).

The Spirit's discipline, reaching far and wide,
Denies the comfort we keep demanding,
But as we take our place in the Crucified (Gal. 2:20),
We find peace past all understanding (Phil. 4:7).

Canaan

Now, as before, a new battle begins
For which we are ill-prepared,
As Satan his fiery darts expends (Eph. 6:16)
To tempt us again to despair.

When he launches his savage attack (1 Pet. 5:8-9)
To regain the ground he has lost,
We are tempted to quit and turn our back
On the warfare and its ultimate cost (Eph. 6:12).

In the battle fierce with strength bereft,
We realize that all is but loss
And retrace our steps to the place we left (1 Cor. 2:14)
As he delivers us alway to the Cross (2 Cor. 4:11).

As our mortal flesh shows our union with him,
Jesus' life will be made manifest,
And the things of this world will ever grow dim,
As we enter into rest (Heb. 4:3).

Though your way seems hopeless and full of fears,
God is handling you in love, dear friend;
No matter how dark your tunnel appears,
Take heart, there is light at the other end.

C. R. Solomon

NINE

Counseling at the Century's End

Compared with the early seventies, there is very little substantive difference in the way some evangelicals approach counseling today. Christian approaches to counseling have proliferated, with some very well-trained and dedicated men and women in the forefront of the movement. There are many books and seminars, but of those who have gained prominence in the development of counseling approaches and have written about them, the common denominator is that their teaching omits the message of the cross of Christ. (If you have read the previous chapters, you will understand that by "the cross" I mean the experience of the believer's death and resurrection with Christ, as described in Romans 6 and elsewhere in the New Testament.)

This does not mean that Christian counselors who do not emphasize this truth do not have God's hand of blessing on their work. However, it is my prayer that God will encourage those who are leaders in the field of counseling to take that final step of teaching the Cross.

The message of the Cross, with its emphasis on death to the power of sin is not a popular message today. Yet I believe that the experienced Cross is the only scriptural way to victory because it is only the cross of Christ, and all that it means, that can deal with the flesh in the life of the believer. Anything short of this results in the strengthening of the flesh, which is a deterrent to solid spiritual growth.

Having said that, it will be apparent to the reader that Spirituotherapy has more in common with *ministries* characterized by teaching the Cross than with the fields of Christian psychology and counseling. Though the message is not new, the introduction of it as a systematic counseling approach is. Down through the centuries, the teaching of believers such as Madame Guyon, Hudson Taylor, Jessie Penn-Lewis, Hannah Whitall Smith, George Mueller, Andrew Murray, Watchman Nee, and a host of others have followed along the same lines.

As one might surmise, over the years people have misunderstood and misrepresented my counseling approach and theological position. Without resorting to name-calling, I would like to correct some impressions you may have received if you have read widely in the field or have attended many seminars. One prominent writer wrote that I teach the annihilation of the personality, and it was reported to me that the same writer held one of my books aloft and declared, "This is a very dangerous book!"

Some have incorrectly inferred and have stated that I teach sinless perfection. Another writer has stated publicly and in writing that I teach, or would not deny, that the believer atones for his own sin. (After being confronted on this, he softened his statement in a later edition of the same book.)

Another writer erroneously holds my position to be that rejection is the reason we must go to the Cross. Others have made erroneous assumptions about what we do, or fail to do, in counseling, and have stated them as facts without ever discussing them with me or a GFI representative. (Some of this is deserved, since I have not written about those things that are common to all good counseling but, rather, have concentrated on those aspects of our counseling that are unique.)

Because of a faulty understanding of "exchanged life" theology, some have said that we teach or foster passivity. Other have reported to me additional statements made in various public gatherings, but I believe I have covered those that might unnecessarily weaken the confidence of the uninformed about my counseling approach. It is for this reason that I have pointed out these allegations rather than attempted to defend the Lord's work. Almost thirty years of ministry and God's hand of blessing in countless lives in this and other countries attest to the validity of this approach.

While not all Christians in the field of psychology would opt for some type of psychotherapy, certainly most of them do, despite the poor results of such treatment. Typically, many of the troublesome symptoms of the mind and emotions are mistakenly diagnosed as "mental illness," and those so afflicted begin the rounds of psychologists and psychiatrists in a vain attempt to meet their needs, either without God or as an "add-on" to their Christian faith. Since "everyone is doing it," mental health has become as acceptable as motherhood, although there is much less understanding about it.

As the problem of mental health becomes an enigma that everyone recognizes and many talk about, there is a frenzy of activity—enormous outlays of money but few permanent results. One young man to whom we ministered had been in a mental-health facility for two years in addition to receiving other treatment. His father's insurance company had paid out a reported $250,000 in medical benefits, but there was little, if any, permanent change in the young man's life. A GFI counselor met with him for three days, and the Holy Spirit did a major work in his life. The young man said that he knew more about himself and the cause of his problem after the first interview than he had in all of his previous treatment.

The "revolving door" syndrome, or recidivism, is a given in mental health endeavors, and as such mental-health professionals must continuously deal with it. Despite their use of many types of psychotherapy, there is little statistical evidence to support the validity of psychotherapy as a treatment modality. In "The Inefficacy of Therapeutic Processes with Adults," an article in *Sources of Gain in Counseling and Psychotherapy,* Hans J. Eynsenck wrote:

> In general, certain conclusions are possible from these data. They fail to prove that psychotherapy, Freudian or otherwise, facilitates the recovery of neurotic patients. They show that roughly two-thirds of a group of neurotic patients will recover or improve to a marked extent within about two years of the onset of their illness, whether they are treated by means of psychotherapy or not.

Despite mounting evidence to the contrary and frank questioning within the ranks of psychotherapists as to the efficacy of their work, their offices are filled with those who are seeking bread but who are, in my opinion, being handed stones.

It is not popular, as I have learned over the years, to challenge traditional psychiatry and psychotherapy with the view that, rather than being an adjunct, a complement, or a supplement, spiritual transformation is the only solution that gives permanent change. It is ironic that some ministers are even less receptive to considering such a claim than psychotherapists are.

Personally, I do not think it coincidental that Freud and Lenin were contemporaries, since both were guided by the god of this world, Satan. Lenin's work provided the foundation for the political, economic, and social revolutions that we have witnessed in this century. Freud's work completed the unholy alliance by bringing into being a counterfeit approach to dealing with soul troubles, an approach that I believe played a major role in undermining the morality of millions around the world.

Few have made the connection between Freud's pronouncements about the centrality of sexuality and the "free sex" of the sixties and seventies and "safe sex" of the eighties and nineties. Still fewer have discerned how his godless influence and the common acceptance of humanistic approaches to psychology have undermined the spiritual fabric of our country, to say nothing of our churches. Freud is the acknowledged grandfather of modern psychology, and liberalism has ridden into some seminaries on the back of psychology. Many seminaries have maintained a thoroughly orthodox theological position, and yet psychology classes espouse ideas about the immaterial makeup of man that are antithetical to those being taught in the theology classes.

I believe there are many Christian psychotherapists who are sound in their faith and fundamental in doctrine. They do much to alleviate the suffering of emotionally disturbed people, returning many of them to a fuller life. But sometimes the apparent success is deceptive. Many times we mistake good psychological adjustment in a Christian for spiritual maturity, and alleviation of symptoms is frequently termed a cure. The person may be active in Christian work, even in the ministry, and yet be out of adjustment spiritually. Psychotherapy helps a person to meet his own needs; to learn more effective ways of thinking, feeling, and behaving; and to develop more adequate defense mechanisms. What the person may be missing is the truth Christ spoke: "Without me ye can do nothing" (John 15:5). As self (or ego, as Freud would define it) grows stronger, there is an increase in pride and a decrease in humility and dependence upon God.

Psychotherapy has as its goal a stronger person. But God's goal for us seems to be dependence on him. Paul wrote: "When I am weak, then am I strong" (2 Cor. 12:10). Anything that teaches us self-reliance, then, is at cross-purposes with the Holy Spirit and is a substitute for his work in our lives.

It is one thing to help a person understand the dynamics of his thoughts, emotions, and behavior, but it is another thing entirely to use psychological principles exclusively to attempt psychological and behavioral change. The underlying presupposition is that if the psychological functioning and behavior are more acceptable, the person will feel better and be changed. In other words, to change the thinking and behavior is to change the person. To some degree this is true, or therapists would no longer be in business. God, however, works on another principle of change—transformation—to change the person so that the behavior can change. God works through the conversion experience and through the transformation that occurs when we enter into union with Christ.

Spirituotherapy does not use the term *mental illness* since by definition it would suggest that the problem is in the mind. While structural or organic anomalies such as brain tumors, brain abnormalities, or defective biochemistry do exist because they are organic rather than functional, we do not generally consider them "mental illness."

For example, sound research has shown that a chemical imbalance exists in the brains of severely depressed patients. For this reason, at Grace Fellowship International we try to work with medical professionals when we deal with such depression. However, to my knowledge no one has proved which comes first—the depression or the chemical imbalance. Since we have seen some patients come out of clinical depression literally overnight, the chemical imbalance—if it did exist in these cases—obviously gave way to the work of the Holy Spirit.

Some who are highly respected in the field of mental health are also rejecting some of the notions about "mental illness." Among these are William Glasser, M.D., Thomas S. Szasz, M.D., and Dr. Garth Wood. In Szasz's preface to his book *The Myth of Mental Illness* (Harper and Row), he writes: "Although mental illness might have been a useful concept in the nineteenth century, today it is scientifically worthless and socially harmful."

Dr. Garth Wood accepts the fact of psychiatric illness but gives the lie to much thinking, feeling, and behavior that has been commonly accepted as the domain of psychotherapy. His book *The Myth of Neurosis* (Harper & Row, 1986) begins:

> In this book I have sought to expose the conspiracy to extend indefinitely the boundaries of mental illness. For far too long people have been led to believe that the person suffering from an excess of life's problems needs "expert" medical and psychotherapeutic intervention, thus allowing the "patient" to qualify for "illness," to the ultimate detriment of his mental equilibrium and often at considerable financial cost. Such a view is dangerous nonsense. If we are not ill then we are well, although we may be unhappy.

Although Dr. Wood does not offer spiritual answers to the dilemma he presents, his "Moral Therapy" is more tenable from a human standpoint than much of what is marketed today under the guise of "mental illness." On the cover flap of his book is this statement:

> Neurosis is a myth. Its bogus status as an illness has stigmatized millions of perfectly normal people whose chief deficiency is their inadequate approach to problems and their unrealistic expectations of what life should bring them. By en-

couraging the damaging "illness excuse," therapists promote the illusion that patients are not responsible for their predicament and, therefore, are powerless to help themselves.

Wood further states: "I define psychiatric illness so that it [neurosis] can be excluded. What remains is individuals who are responsible for their predicament, slaves to neither their environment nor their brain biochemistry, and who are therefore free, with support, to change themselves for the better."

In his book *Reality Therapy* (Harper & Row, 1975), Dr. William Glasser also rejects the concept of mental illness. His basic tenet is that bizarre behavior is merely an ineffective attempt to meet one's needs and that one person must meet his needs through another person. In his words:

At all times in our lives we must have at least one other person who cares about us and whom we care for ourselves. If we do not have this essential person, we will not be able to fulfill our basic needs. One characteristic is essential in the other person: he must be in touch with reality himself and able to fulfill his own needs in the world.

There seems to be a contradiction here, however. How would one find a person who is able to fulfill his own needs if everyone has to have some other person to do this?

This, too, is the basic premise of Spirituotherapy. The prime difference is that the person who meets our needs is the Lord Jesus Christ—not a human therapist. If Glasser's book were read with this significant substitution, it would approximate the approach of Spirituotherapy. While denying that mental aberrations constitute mental illness, both Glasser and Szasz would endorse a type of human therapy.

Although the problem is ultimately spiritual in nature, the obvious manifestation is through psychological and behavioral symptoms. In his book *The Crisis in Psychiatry and Religion* (D. Van Nostrand Co., 1961), Dr. O. Hobart Mowrer takes a strong stand in favor of a spiritual emphasis in meeting the needs of those who are in emotional and mental distress. He wrote: "If religious leaders had been deeply involved in the care and redemption of seriously disturbed persons for the past century, instead of systematically "referring" such persons, there would have been no Freud and no necessity for a Tillich or a Fosdick to try and legitimize him."

Even though the symptoms are mental and emotional, and classifying such symptoms can aid our communication about them, to attempt therapy in the realm of the psyche or mind is folly since it is merely symptomatic treatment. Some symptoms respond in varying degrees to psychotherapy, although the source of the problem is seldom, if ever, touched on in the process. In Spirituotherapy, there is no benefit to offering different diagnoses from a psychological standpoint. This is merely a method of classifying symptoms. Since the source of the problem is ultimately spiritual in nature, it is infinitely more important to determine the spiritual state of the individual. The person rarely cares which particular psychological phenomenon has been his plight, as long as he discovers how to unload it. Some people coming to Grace Fellowship International have been labeled during previous visits to psychotherapists. Some were given little hope for recovery, and others were told outright that they would never be any better. But God did not honor such prophecy.

We have seen God deliver many people from various symptomatic ailments that now pass for mental illness or emotional disturbance. Some of the more common ones are depression, anorexia nervosa, bulimia, homosexuality (which was given the honored status of an alternate lifestyle by psychiatry in 1973), obsessive-compulsive behavior, obsessive thoughts, behavioral problems, addictions, and most other types of so-called neurotic disturbances. In addition, many who have had psychotic episodes have been set free. It seems that some who have been diagnosed and treated for paranoid schizophrenia have definite organicity and will have to be continuously treated with medication unless God chooses to do a physical healing as well. We have not found chronic schizophrenics to be good candidates for spiritual counseling in an outpatient setting.

The counselor in Spirituotherapy is not a therapist but a spiritual director. The therapy is accomplished by the Master Therapist, the

Holy Spirit. His work within the human spirit results in deliverance from psychological symptoms caused by spiritual maladjustment. This is not to say that all psychological difficulties have a spiritual genesis. Many, if not most, of these stem from early childhood, as we discussed in chapter 1, or from some significant trauma. Psychology is beneficial in understanding some of the behavior that follows, but the use of psychology in treatment is often counterproductive. When a person is unwilling to have God's answers, or is unaware of God's answers, psychotherapy is the only recourse for symptomatic relief. But it is not the answer to the problem.

God did not promise to meet our emotional and mental needs through a counselor, psychologist, or psychiatrist, just as he did not promise to meet our visceral or physiological need through a physician. He did say, "My God shall supply all your need according to his riches in glory by Christ Jesus" (Phil. 4:19). Spirituotherapy takes Paul's position literally, unequivocally, and unapologetically, and trusts God to honor his Word and perform a miraculous deliverance in the life of each person who comes for counseling.

If the counselor is to be able, with conviction, to tell a person that God will supply all his needs, then the counselor must provide the example by casting himself completely upon the Lord even in the matter of salary. The commitment of the counselor must pervade every area of his life if he is to be a guide and example to those with whom he shares Christ. This is in direct contrast to that of conventional psychotherapy. In many forms of therapy, the therapist is not required to have experienced what he prescribes. And in some approaches to therapy, the therapist is not encouraged to be congruent in the relationship but to maintain the professional facade of the therapist-client relationship. Records are replete with cases where the therapist is unable to meet his own needs. Statistics show that for many years the suicide rate for psychiatrists has been the highest of any profession—mute evidence to the failure of the therapeutic climate to meet the deepest needs of people—either clients or therapists.

God's purpose in redemption was not just to forgive our sins and help us live with our problems by harnessing our flesh to "work for him." Christ came not just to reconcile us to himself but to save us from ourselves by his life (Rom. 5:10). He came to give us life more abundantly (John 10:10). It is estimated that 90 percent of all Christians never experience the abundant or victorious life, so they do not understand how deep psychological problems can be resolved by letting the Lord Jesus Christ manifest his life in them, rather than resorting to human therapy. The same is true of many pastors, Christian psychologists, and psychiatrists. Although Christian in their orientation to life, they resort to therapy as a means of showing people how their needs can be met.

Even in Christian educational institutions, it has become commonly accepted to relegate the treatment of mental and emotional disturbances to the "professionals," which means that many believers are referred outside the church for the solution to problems of the soul that only the Holy Spirit, working through yielded believers, can resolve. Thus, the turf is neatly carved out to the satisfaction of both disciplines. The behavioral sciences are more than happy to have this lucrative referral source, and those trained in theology do not have to deal with sticky situations of behavior. In fact, many escape the acid test of the efficacy of their particular theological position by ascribing to another discipline the responsibility for treating those in soul trouble.

A Model of the Field of Counseling

The chart in diagram 19 might aid the reader in comparing and contrasting what typically happens in the arena of counseling. Although we could cover the behavioral sciences more thoroughly by addressing the fields of psychology and psychiatry, the chart restricts itself to the arena of counseling. It is assumed that counselors do not handle to the same depth problems usually treated in psychotherapy, but the line of demarcation between psychotherapy and counseling is often blurred.

In this particular chart, the secular module includes psychiatry, psychotherapy, and counseling so far as the presuppositions are concerned. The four major forces listed are Psychoanalytic (Freud), Behavior Modification (Skinner, Watson), Phenomenological (Rog-

DIAGRAM 19

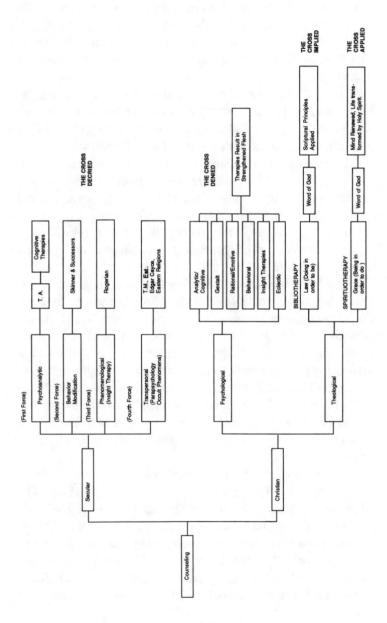

ers), and Transpersonal (Edgar Casey, et all). There have been numerous offshoots of each of these, but just a few are shown. The fourth force, Transpersonal, or the occult in its various forms, is the most rapidly proliferating at the present time. Naturally, the Cross in all its dimensions is *decried* by therapy that is based on godless presuppositions.

We have divided the Christian approaches to counseling into those that are primarily psychological and those that are primarily theological. The psychological approaches are rooted in the secular approaches, with the exception of the Transpersonal, which is based largely on the occult and Eastern religions. While those in Christian psychology would utilize Scripture and scriptural principles in varying degrees, some type of psychotherapy is taking place since that is the work of the psychologist, whose work is consistent with his training and title. As such, the power of the Cross to release suffering people from mental and emotional disturbances without the use of therapy is *denied.*

The analytical/cognitive approaches trace their origins to Freud, even though some would deny much of Freud's theory. These deal primarily with the thought processes, as the name implies. The Gestalt approach is heavily freighted with emotional content and was pioneered by Fritz Pearles. Albert Ellis combined the cognitive and the emotional approaches and called his variety of psychotherapy Rational Emotive Therapy. The behavioral approach is rooted in the Behavior Modification of Skinner, while the insight therapies trace their roots to Carl Rogers and his client-centered approach. The Eclectic approach is sort of a smorgasbord, taking a little of anything that works.

Distinctions within the theological approaches are harder to make, except that they might be grouped under the headings of law and grace. Approaches that look to the experienced cross of Christ as the method and goal are under the heading of grace, while those that emphasize self-effort with the Lord's help would come under the category of law. Those in the law group would teach that one must *do* in order to *be,* while those in the grace category would teach that we must *be* in order to *do.* Although the Word of God is foundational to both, in the case of the law approach, scriptural principles are applied by counselor and counselee without the Cross having become a reality. Change may take place in the life, but *exchange* does not.

It is possible for counseling to be Bible-centered without being Christ-centered or Cross-centered. Christ-centered counseling (grace) will always be biblical, but biblical counseling is not always Christ-centered as we have defined it throughout the book. Any approach that does not make the experience of the Cross or the exchanged life central to its method and goal might be categorized under the heading of Bibliotherapy, while those that inculcate the message of the life in Christ are here called Spirituotherapy. While this chart is not exhaustive, it might help the reader to assess methods of counseling and remove the mask from that which, though thoroughly biblical, strengthens the flesh because the Cross is *implied* rather than *applied.* I believe these are the only two alternatives: It is either flesh or Spirit.

If I understand the Bible correctly, the abundant life and anxiety are mutually exclusive, as Paul wrote: "Be careful for nothing. . . . And the peace of God, which passeth all understanding, shall keep your hearts and minds through Christ Jesus" (Phil. 4:6-7).

All Christians enjoy peace *with* God through redemption, but relatively few enjoy the peace *of* God. It is this peace that the neurotic and psychotic person is desperate to know. Likewise, it is this peace that the so-called well-adjusted person needs, even though he usually does not understand that he has a problem until his comfortable world begins to come apart at the seams. In either case, the discipline of adversity, faithfully administered by our sovereign Lord, is often necessary before we begin to seek him with all our hearts (Ps. 119:17; Jer. 29:13).

Abundant life, or the Spirit-filled life, is not God's portion for a chosen few. God intends that all of his children go beyond knowing Christ as Savior and Lord to knowing him as *life.* It is to this end that this book is dedicated. It is not written just to the professionals in the field of theology and the helping professions but to any searching soul who sincerely wants to know the Lord Jesus Christ as "all, and in all" (Col. 3:11).

Suggestions for
Additional Reading

V. Raymond Edman. *They Found the Secret*. Grand Rapids, Mich.: Zondervan, 1984.

Bob George. *Classic Christianity*. Eugene, Oreg.: Harvest House, 1992.

Bill Gillham. *Lifetime Guarantee*. Eugene, Oreg.: Harvest House, 1993.

Roy Hession. *Calvary Road*. Fort Washington, Penn.: Christian Literature Crusade, 1992.

F. J. Huegel. *Bone of His Bone*. Beaumont, Tex.: Seedsowers, 1997.

L. E. Maxwell. *Born Crucified*. Chicago: Moody Press, 1984.

Steve McVey. *Grace Walk*. Eugene, Oreg.: Harvest House, 1995.

Andrew Murray. *Abide in Christ*. Fort Washington, Penn.: Christian Literature Crusade, 1992.

Watchman Nee. *The Normal Christian Life*. Fort Washington, Penn.: Christian Literature Crusade, 1979.

Stephen Olford. *Not I but Christ*. Wheaton, Ill.: Crossway, 1997.

Ruth Paxson. *Life on the Highest Plane*. Grand Rapids, Mich.: Kregel, 1996.

Jessie Penn-Lewis. *The Centrality of the Cross*. Fort Washington, Penn.: Christian Literature Crusade, 1993.

Hannah W. Smith. *The Christian's Secret of a Happy Life*. Uhrichsville, Ohio: Barbour, 1996.

Miles Stanford. *The Complete Green Letters*. Grand Rapids, Mich.: Zondervan, 1983.

Howard Taylor, Mary G. Taylor, and Gregg Lewis. *Hudson Taylor's Spiritual Secret*. Chicago: Moody Press, 1981.

Jack Taylor. *The Key to Triumphant Living*. Beaumont, Tex.: Seedsowers, 1996.

W. Ian Thomas. *The Saving Life of Christ*. Grand Rapids, Mich.: Zondervan, 1989.

A. W. Tozer. *The Best of A. W. Tozer*. Camp Hill, Penn.: Christian Publications, Inc., 1995.

Charles Trumbull. *Victory in Christ*. Fort Washington, Penn.: Christian Literature Crusade, 1992.

Michael Wells. *Sidetracked in the Wilderness*. Grand Rapids, Mich.: Revell, 1991.

About the Author

Charles Solomon was born at the beginning of the Great Depression and suffered both economic and emotional deprivation. The pressures of his struggle with the resulting emotional conflict, his early marriage, and his position in aerospace engineering brought on psychosomatic ailments, a near nervous breakdown, and thoughts of suicide.

When Dr. Solomon was thirty-five, the Holy Spirit made Galatians 2:20 a reality in his life. He still believed that death was the only way out, but now he knew that it was understanding the death to sin that comes from identifying with Christ in *his* death and resurrection. In 1967 God called Dr. Solomon to develop and pioneer an approach to counseling that has come to be known as "exchanged life counseling." In response to that call, he started a full-time counseling ministry in 1970 at the age of forty. He is the author of several books, including *The Ins and Out of Rejection, Gems and Jargon,* and *Handbook to Happiness in Verse.* He and his wife, Sue, have three children and five grandchildren and live in Pigeon Forge, Tennessee.